Open Fields & (

(The Life of a Cotsv

by
Peter Stayt

Peter and Mary Stayt 1993 with a Championship cup.

Published for the
Stayt Family
by
Reardon Publishing
56 Upper Norwood Street, Leckhampton
Cheltenham, Glos, GL53 0DU
www.reardon.co.uk

Written by Peter Stayt

Captain Millais' tribute to Peter Stayt

Peter has gone - after over a year in and out of hospitals, with leukaemia, borne with uncomplaining courage. He and Mary have been part of my life and family for over fifty years. He was a great friend, a great gentleman and a great man. He knew, and was a friend of, and admired by, hundreds of people in the Cotswolds. Someone has gone who cannot be replaced. They don't make them like him anymore.

Raoul Millais
Westcote Manor.

Acknowledgements.

The Stayt Family would like to thank Westcote History Society for help and encouragement in publishing these memoirs, especially Connie Fisher, and Pamela Rouse for sorting and typing up Peter's manuscripts.

Thanks are also expressed to Eileen Hayes for some of the photographs.

A percentage of the profits from this book
will be donated to Leukaemia Charities.

ISBN 1 873877 40 4

Layout and Design
Nicholas Reardon

Cover photo
Paddy Burns, Swell Hill 1946
Captain, Toby and Benny pulling a 2 furrow Lister Cockshut plough.

Printed by
Stoate & Bishop (Printers) Ltd
Cheltenham

Foreword

As a small boy I thought Mum's kitchen must be magic to attract such funny and nice people. On winter days especially, after Dad had fed the animals, I would sit and wait to see who would come. There would be at least two at a time and I would sit and listen to the stories they would tell, always on the bright and funny side. They made life seem fantastic.

Now I wish I had taped some of their stories because most of these men have passed on, men who never spoke ill of anybody or ran anybody down. I am so glad Dad managed to put pen to paper and record some of his life.

Dad was such a strong and fit man, always on the go. It was not like him to stay indoors, let alone go to bed, so when he took to his bed for days we knew he must have been very poorly. The doctor took blood samples. When the results came back they rushed Dad straight to Cheltenham Hospital, as he was diagnosed with leukaemia. Dad had two very large doses of chemotherapy. This was very difficult for him and drove him mad being shut in a room for months at a time, the first month in a room with no window!

It was so nice to get him home, even though he was only half the man that went into hospital. He soon started to pick up with Mum's cooking and T.L.C. and was walking to see his beloved horses again.

A few months went by and he was going for long walks and helping to raise money for the Lillbrook Ward at the Hospital. By this time he had started to write a bit about his life, just a page a day. His blood tests were encouraging and looked good.

Then leukaemia stuck again with a vengeance and ravaged him within a few weeks. He passed away peacefully with all the family present on April 19th 1998.

We miss him dearly and, as the days go by and things happen, I realize what a good man and special dad he was to me. I thought it would be tough, and perhaps sad, to read Dad's book. But I find it a good tonic to realize what a happy and interesting life he had, and I hope our readers will feel the same

Tom Stayt (Peter's son),
Church Westcote 1999.

Part 1
Early Years

My parents were married in 1922. My father was from a local farming family. My mother came from Gloucester and was working in the Talbot Hotel in Stow. Dad's father, Tom, was born in Church Westcote, one of nine children, seven boys and two girls. Grandad Tom went to Canada in about 1870 where Dad was born. They came back to England in about 1890 and rented Swell Hill Farm which belonged to Grandad's eldest brother, William, who had emigrated to South Africa.

Dad 1914. Royal Gloucestershire Hussars

Dad joined the Royal Gloucestershire Hussars in 1914 and served in the Middle East where he was wounded and pieces of shrapnel were under his skin for the rest of his life. At the end of the 14 -18 war he returned to Swell Hill and worked with Grandad for a while as a shepherd. During this time he was trying to get up to a barn owl's nest when the old bird attacked him and removed his right eye with her claws. Dad had a glass eye for the rest of his life. He learnt to shoot left handed and we said that he could see more with one eye than most people with two!

After they married my parents moved to Heath Farm where Dad was farm manager for a Mr. Ted "Tricky" Smith. This is where my brother Reg was born on December 12th 1927. Soon after they took a council small holding between Shipton and Leafield, known as Langley Holding, and this is where I was born on July 12th 1930. The only thing I can remember about Langley Holding was a little fox terrier called Nipper being run over and Dad wrapping him in his old army overcoat, but he soon died and was buried in the garden.

Swell Hill
By 1933 Grandad Tom had got bad on his legs so we moved back to Swell Hill and Dad took on the tenancy. Grandad and Granny lived in part of the house until Grandad's death in 1936. Then Granny moved to Stonesfield to live with her relations.

Swell Hill was a farm of 210 acres. Over half of this was arable and all the work was done with horses. My first recollections were of three men working on the farm. There was an old man with a large drooping moustache who was known as "Carter", a lad of about 15 who was called "The Boy" and a nice man called Jack who looked after Grandad's cob and Dad's riding horse, and did a bit of gardening and odd jobs. He would take me with him if he went anywhere in the trap or carry me in front of him on Grandad's cob.

Mum and Dad at Swell Hill 1925

Grandad Tom

Grandad Tom was quite a character. He loved all country pursuits and was a great cricketer in his day. He loved horses and being about six feet two inches tall and weighing about eighteen stone he needed a big horse to carry him. He hunted when the hounds were in the district. He was a good shot, kept ferrets and terriers and always had a good gun dog, although he never kept a running dog. He said they chased game off your land. He was president and top judge at the Cotswold Coursing Club. All his sporting activities left little time for farming. That didn't seem to worry him. In fact the farm was neglected if any sport was available.

(Guts & Gaiters) 1930 my Grandfather Tom Stayt

He smoked a pipe endlessly and liked a drop of whisky. All in all he enjoyed life. I spent most of my time in his company from 1933 to his death in 1936. Grandad was not too good on his legs, so walked at about the same speed as me, a four or five year old. I went with him to shoot rabbits and pigeons and wait for wild duck when they came to feed on the stubbles from nearby Eyeford Lakes. We would also set rabbit wires and he always had vermin traps set, to catch rats, stoats, weasels etc. He also encouraged us boys into mischief, nothing really serious. One thing I remember was him taking Gramma's boiled egg out of the saucepan and putting a china egg in its place. Granny was not amused. Grandad chuckled all day.

Grandad always went to Stow Thursday evenings to collect the groceries and catch up with the news. He stabled his horse at the Talbot Hotel and after going round the shops ordering goods he would have them delivered to the Talbot before eight o'clock which was when he set out for home. Among the groceries was always eight ounces of tobacco for Grandad's pipe. Well, one Thursday evening Grandad and his cronies were sitting round the fire telling yarns and getting quite merry. The grocer's boy had delivered the large box of provisions. Some wag near the box took Grandad's parcel of tobacco from the top of the box, gave it to the man sitting next to him saying, "Pass it on and put it on the fire". Well Grandad was nearest the fire and threw the parcel on. When the paper began to burn he could see what he had done. "Hey that's my baccy" he shouted. "Well you put it on the fire!" they all laughed.

Another time they had all met at the "White Hart". I think a Mrs. Groves was landlady there in those days, and the farmers would gather there on Thursdays-market day. Some of them stayed in the pub most of the day! On this particular day a local farmer had a litter of young pigs in his horse float at the back of the pub and had several likely customers out to see them and to make him an offer. He had not sold the pigs and was still in the bar at six o'clock. One of the crowd suggested he stayed to supper as the landlady was roasting a sucking pig for them. He agreed to stay and after the meal said it was the best pork he had ever eaten. They said "It should be. It was one of yours!" Earlier in the day one of them had got a pig from his float and taken it to the butcher Blan Febry who had his slaughter house across the road next to the Queen's Head. He had killed and dressed the pig and given it back to Mrs. Groves to cook.

Another story from the "White Hart" was about a Mr. Bartlet who got drunk on occasions. When he had a session he really got paralytic. Instead of putting his pony in the trap to take him home two men got between the shafts and were covered with a horse blanket. When Mr. Bartlet got into the trap and said "Get on" to the pony, they pushed the trap backwards down the yard and tipped him out of the back onto the muck heap!

As I said before Grandad was a great sportsman. He even made a tennis court when his family were young. All of them played tennis and Grandad put up trophies and arranged tournaments. He also ran sparrow shoots and skittle matches. Anything to get away from work! There were five sons and one daughter, all of whom emigrated except Dad and one brother, Will, cousin Robin and David's father. Grandad, not surprisingly, suffered with gout, which didn't help his temper at times. He died in Bourton Hospital in 1936 and I missed him very much.

Farewell to Jack

Soon after Grandad's death Jack finished working at Swell Hill. The last time I remember seeing him was one Saturday. He took the big Gloucestershire wagon and three horses down to the wood and Dad helped him to put a big load on, topped by wood faggots, leaving a small place in the front for my brother and myself to ride. We went with Jack to his cottage about three miles away and after he had unloaded the wood his wife gave us some dinner. I can remember riding home in the bottom of the wagon, covered by Jack's big overcoat and with a tummy full of hot stew. I did not wake up till we were home. I don't think I saw Jack again and I should think the wood was a retirement present.

Early School Days

I was walking to Swell School, a mile and a half each way, taking sandwiches with me, usually home cured bacon. I left home about 8.15 in the morning and never got home till about 4.30pm. In the winter it was dark at both times. The infants teacher was Miss Morse, an elderly lady who rode a very upright bicycle from Slaughter every day. She ate her lunch with us. I think she was a vegetarian because she always ate a slice of bread and butter and an apple. She would look down her nose at my fat bacon! The head teacher was Mrs. Blake who lived in the school house and her husband kept a lot of laying hens and also hives of bees. Mrs. Blake was very strict and caned both boys and girls alike, even the infants. If they were sent to the headmistress they knew what to expect! We all had a third of a pint of milk a day. This, two of the boys fetched from Mr. Oughton's farm just across the road from the school and we paid two and a half pence per week. This milk was straight from the cows, not having been treated in any way. In the winter the milk was stood round the tortoise stove, the only heating in the whole school. When I was attending the little school Miss Morse had a young assistant, a Miss Howman. She would sit close to me with her right arm round me, guiding my hand and teaching me to draw pothooks and ABC. I remember how nice she smelt, so different from Miss Morse's wintergreen oils. They also taught both boys and girls to sew, make table mats with raffia and sew on buttons. At home I spent most of my time with Dad or the carter. I had to be out of doors. My brother Reg had his head in a book most of the time. He did help on the farm now and then, but mostly under protest.

My brother Reg and I. 1936.

Pranks at Swell School

At Swell School I would take my sandwiches to Tucker's house at dinner time and his mother, Mrs. Hathaway, would give me a cup of cocoa. Tucker and me had started school the same day and become firm friends. Well, one day Tucker and me got playing with his toy cars in a heap of sand. His mum had gone to work and we decided not to go back to school that afternoon. We just carried on playing until going home time. Next morning Mrs. Smith, who was the head teacher, called us out in front of the class and asked for an explanation. I said, "We had to take a sow to the boar for my Dad". I suppose I thought that would embarrass her and we wouldn't hear any more about it. The trouble was Mrs. Smith used to walk to Swell Hill about once a week to buy eggs from Mum. She chose that evening to go for eggs. Was I in trouble! The next morning Tucker and me had to write on the blackboard 2 x 10 = 20. That was the amount of hours we had to stay in after school. So each evening we stayed behind one hour for twenty days. We tried all sorts of things, like telling Mrs. Smith that she needn't stay with us, we could lock up when we left. She just smiled and said she liked staying with us.

The parson, Revd. McCleary, used to take us for scripture lessons once a week. One day he was telling us that religion is the food for the soul just as porridge is food for the body. Tucker and me weren't paying attention, so the Vicar suddenly shouts, "Hathaway, what did I say was food for the soul?" "Porridge Sir", said Tucker.

Another time two of us had been scrumping the vicar's apples during the lunch hour-he had the best apples in the parish. He came into the school in the afternoon and asked if we had seen anyone taking his apples. Of course we hadn't. "I'm very surprised you Walmesly and you Stayt didn't see anyone because I found two caps with your names in under the trees". He then produced the two caps from behind his back, but he didn't take any further action.

Next door to the school lived a Mr. and Mrs. Tom Clark. She was not keen on letting us have our ball back if it went over the wall. Now her wash house was just over the wall, with the top of the boiler chimney about six feet high. Monday morning was wash day, so when she got the boiler going one of the bigger boys would climb up and place a piece of cardboard over the top of the chimney. (She couldn't see the top from her side. She had to go out into the road to see). Well, when we heard the door open the piece of cardboard would be removed. You would hear her say to someone in the road "My copper fire will not go today. I expect the wind's in the wrong direction". As soon as she went back in the cardboard was replaced and so on!

Saturday Mornings

Saturday mornings were something special - no school for one thing and my friend Tucker Hathaway came to play with me. He, like me, was fond of horses. Sometimes I would go to meet him half way to Swell on Saturday. Sometimes I would go all the way. On one occasion I went all the way to Swell taking "Mick", Dad's terrier with me. Now Mick was scared of nothing or no one! Doctor Leslie King had a white bull terrier called "Robin" which had attacked several dogs and bitten several people. Well, as we passed the doctor's gates Robin looked out and growled. That was enough for Mick. He was straight in there and all hell was let loose. After a few minutes all went quiet and someone came to me and said how sorry they were and what a shame about my little dog, when out came Mick as cocky as ever with his head held high. We later learnt that Mick had grabbed Robin by his front foot and crunched it. Robin was seen later, and carried his front foot for a long time. In the summer Tucker and me would be out of doors playing in the woods or helping Dad, but in the winter we would be in the big stone barn playing with our toys, or grooming the horses or calves.

My Sixth Birthday

When I was six years old I had a tea party in the stone barn. I think all of the children from Swell School were invited and a lot more beside. Some came on foot, some in parents' cars and some on ponies. I remember Frank Gaden's three children coming in a pony and trap with Audrey the eldest at the reins and Michael and Elizabeth sitting beside her. I remember Dad helping to put the pony in the carthorse stable with an armful of hay. After the usual tea of jellies, cake etc., we had a giant game of hide and seek, which went on until quite late. Then there was a bag of sweets to take home. It was a good job it was July and light evenings, as I think it was about ten o'clock before they all went home.

Coursing

Another big occasion was a coursing meeting, where about thirty people met at Swell Hill and they had about twenty running dogs between them. I remember someone taking me in a horse and trap to see the hounds and hares. Then they came back to the farm for lunch. The cart shed had been emptied and trestle tables were put up and were loaded with all kinds of pies and cold meats and a lot of bottles. The men were mostly dressed in tweed jackets and breeches with gaiters or stockings. There was a lot of betting as to who had the fastest dog. Reg and myself were given quite a few shillings and half crowns just for being there. I should think this was about 1937.

Clem Timms

Our hero at the time was a man called Clem Timms. He lived at Chalk Hill about two miles from us. He kept a lot of big heavy horses which he hired to the council for hauling stone and chippings, also for tar spraying and road sweeping. Clem Timms also did timber hauling with horses, drawing huge trees to the railway stations at Stow, Bourton or Moreton. He would come by our farm early in the morning with his man, Wally, and about eight or ten horses, usually pulling two iron-tyred timber wagons. Anyone who had a difficult or unbroken horse would let Clem have it for a week or two. It would never be any more trouble. Hauling timber was the toughest job a horse could have and the men were just as tough.

We had an old mare that was past heavy work. She had bad feet. Her name was Ginger. Tucker and myself would take her into the wood and pretend to be Clem Timms, pulling small dead branches with her. We would take some sandwiches with us and a bottle of lemonade. We would sit on a log and eat while Ginger dozed in the sunshine. What more could two eight year olds want!

Working on the Farm

Of course it was not all play. There were times like potato planting and haymaking, harvest and getting the potatoes up when we had to work, but there always seemed to be some fun even on the busiest days. When we were haymaking the teas were brought out by Mum and the carter's wife. There was cheese and home-made jam, home-made butter, scones and cakes. We sat in the shade of a wagonload of hay, while the horses munched at a pile of new hay. During tea there was always much leg pulling and teasing. This seemed to make the work easier when we all started again.

When we got the potatoes up Dad would light a small fire on the headland, usually with some broken hurdles. When there was a good heap of hot ashes he would cook some large potatoes. My, they did taste good! They were usually black on the outside and I don't suppose we would have eaten them indoors, but they tasted marvellous on a cold October day out on top of the Cotswold Hills.

Dad usually had a barrel of cider on tap. This came from Shepton Mallet in Somerset and was very strong. After it was delivered it would be trammed - that was put on a bench and a tap put in. Then it was left for a week or so to settle. During this time a small hole was left in the top of the barrel to let the gasses out. Well, one year Reg and myself got a long wheat straw and took it in turns sucking cider up the straw. We both became ill and were sent to bed. I can't remember if the cause of the illness was ever discovered!

Threshing was another event. There were eight or ten ricks of corn to thresh. The first was a rick of winter wheat. This was to get some seed wheat to plant in October to harvest the next year, and the straw to thatch the other corn ricks. We usually had two days threshing at the end of September or the beginning of October. One day was a wheat rick, the other was oats to get some feed for the horses and cattle as well as the sheep. The rest of the corn was threshed after Christmas. Dad always had Ernie Bartlet's thresher from Upper Slaughter. He used a big steam engine to drive the drum. When they were moving from farm to farm the engine pulled the drum and either the straw trusser or the chaff cutter. If you wanted both you had to fetch one or the other. If you fetched the straw trusser one horse was enough, but the chaff cutter needed three horses if you had any hills to go up.

A threshing consisted of about ten people,. Two men usually came with the machine, then there was Dad and the carter. One of the engine men's wives would come to cut the bonds, that's the strings that tied the sheaves. Then there were two other men who followed the machine from farm to farm. David Williams was one. He was a jobbing gardener and grave digger. The other was Laughing Harry who pretended to be the village idiot, but in fact cashed in on his speaking disability. He would do the dirtiest job threshing, taking the chaff and rubbish away, but made sure he had an extra half crown a day for doing it! The other three men would be borrowed from neighbouring farms. About a week before threshing Dad would buy two tons of steam coal for the engine. Then, when you started threshing you needed a good supply of water as well. I suppose an engine driving a drum would use about two cwt of coal and about fifty gallons of water a day. Later on, when the war started, Mr. Bartlett sold his steam engine and bought a big International Tractor.

Horses-Toby

Up until 1945 our life was around horses. The first horse in my life was Grandad's cob, Toby. He was big and black with a white blaze on his face. He was always fit. He lived in his stable and was fed mostly chaffed clover, hay and oats, with a bit of hay at night which was damped down with water to prevent dust. Toby worked every day. Grandad Tom rode regularly and drove Toby in the trap-some journeys would be twenty miles or more! Toby also pulled the horserake at haymaking time and did a bit of horse hoeing. When I hear people say their horse is tired I wonder if they know how to feed them. I always think a horse is an athlete. You never cut down their food, but give them enough work to burn it up. There are all sorts of patent foods today, most of which are belly fill. All a horse needs today are hay, oats and clean water. I have proved it!

After Grandad's death and Granny leaving, a man came and said he had orders to fetch Grandad's cob, Toby. Dad refused to let him go, knowing that Granny had no use for him. The man left, but came back a week later with a solicitor and a letter of authority and poor old Toby was led away. We heard later that he was pulling a fruit and veg van round Oxford. Dad never spoke to his mother again and he never used the trap again.

Ponies from Stow Fair

Dad would buy two pony colts at Stow Fair. We would take an old mare to Stow and once we got away from the other horses, these ponies would follow her back to Swell Hill. As soon as they were two years old Jack Walker, the horse vet, would castrate them. Then we would start leading them about and getting them quiet. Then a chap in his late teens from Swell, called Bush Fessy, would get on them for the first time. Although he was bucked off many times he always landed on his feet and got straight back on again. As time went on and they got quieter Reg and myself would ride them. After a while they would be sold and we had two more young ones again.

The last pony I broke in, I was about twelve at the time, was a chestnut roan with some hair on his legs and I was getting on really well with him, riding most evenings after school. Well, I was pushing my bike up the hill on the way home from school, when I met another boy on my pony coming down the hill. He just looked at me and said "This is my pony now". When I got home there were tears. Dad had been made a good offer for Tom, so he had sold him. "There are two more youngsters in the field" he said. It was no good. I had lost interest in riding ponies.

Working with the horses

Everything we did every day was connected to horses. The first job in the morning was to let the working horses in from the field for their first feed of chaff and corn.

When they were in full work they had about fifteen pounds of oats a day. Then, to see the sheep you could either walk, ride a horse or take the horse and float. When the sheep were being fed in winter you took the float. You also took a half hundred weight to tie the horse to. Our horses didn't like standing in the middle of a field in the cold, when their friends were in the stable eating, so if you didn't tie your float horse he was soon gone without you!

The team of three horses went out to land work at about half past seven, which usually left two in the stable. One would be an older horse which didn't mind standing about and doing odd jobs. The other was probably the float horse. These two would make another team for Dad to do the harrowing or such.

If Mother went to Cheltenham, which was about once a month, Dad would take her to the top of Slaughter Lane to catch Young's bus, and meet her again about 6.30 in the evening. This was done with the float. Also fetching and taking to and from Stow or the station was done in the float. In fact horse power was the only power we knew up to Dad's death in 1948.

When I go to horse shows or gymkhanas these days I often hear young people telling their friends all the bad things about their horses. "Oh this horse pulls like mad. I have to use a gag" or "My horse is a crib biter", or something else is faulty about their mount. Now, when I was young if anyone asked about the horse I was riding or driving it was the best horse I had ever had. Father had lectured us on this. Also we only used snaffle bits. They are the softest on a horse's mouth. Dad would say "If you can't manage him in a snaffle, get off and let someone ride him who can", meaning himself. Dad always told us "If a horse is running away with you drop one rein and hang on the other with both hands". This pulls the horse's head round and he doesn't go anywhere. It works.

More about Horses

I always had a soft spot for horses, especially cart horses. The first ones I remember were Kit, Violet, Captain and Dick. Kit was more of a cob, lighter on the leg than a cart horse and able to trot in the float for going to market etc. The others were hairy legged cart horses.

Captain and Collier with my Dad.
Single furrow ball plough, 1933.

In about 1938 Dad employed a new carter. He came from Herefordshire. His name was Mr. Morris but he was known as "The Carter". At about this time Dad bought three younger horses, Short, Joey and Punch. Short and Joey were Carter's favourite pair, and when he was ploughing with three horses abreast Punch was his third horse. Carter Morris was a good man with horses and was very kind to them. In fact, in his time as carter we had several run away. Dad said it was because they had too much corn and not enough work! I remember telling tales to Dad that the carter was stealing the best clover hay for his horses. This hay was set aside for the young calves. Dad's reply was "I know he is but if he thinks I don't know he wont give it to them in waste".

At about this time Dad took one or two young horses to break for other people so we had plenty of horsepower. I was often sent to do a carting job or some harrowing with one of the quieter ones. One of my favourite jobs on Saturday mornings was to take two or three bags of corn to the neighbours to be ground into flour for the pigs. Dad would shut the horse in the cart, load the bags, help me up and I would drive to the next farm, where they would unload the bags and grind the flour while I played with their children. Then they would load me and the bags and send me home again. My, how proud I was if I met someone who I knew!

I must mention Ginger. She was a chestnut mare, who had spent most of her life pulling a roadsweeper in a city. When she came to us via the knacker man she had very bad feet through working on the roads and standing in stables at night. Dad treated her feet every day and left her out in the field on the soft grass. It was not long before she was able to do light carting jobs. She was very willing, but she was never asked to do heavy work. I should think I was eight when Ginger came and I spent many happy hours just grooming her and putting Grandad's trap harness on her and cleaning the brasses and trying to plait her tail like Carter did with his horses. I had to stand in the wheelbarrow to reach, but Ginger never moved a foot. I'm sure she understood. I don't know what happened at the end. I came home from school and Mum said "Poor old Ginger's gone". I was too upset to ask what had happened. She must have been very old.

Hunting

I always liked watching the foxhounds at work. I've only been hunting on a horse on three occasions. I prefer to go on foot. You can see a lot more. When I am watching hounds I don't notice who is riding the horses. I love to watch the hounds working out the line and watch the horses jumping, and, of course, see a fox creep away up some wall or hedgerow, unless he's a bad fox, that is one that's been stealing chickens or lambs. I don't tell the huntsman. I let the hounds work the line out for themselves. Most followers on horseback never see a fox, let alone see one killed. When I was six I was standing in the "Old Cover" at Swell Hill when the hounds killed their fox right by me. The Master, Lord Ashton of Hyde, blooded me, that is put some fox blood on my face. This may seem disgusting to some people, but it is an honour bestowed on the first person at a kill. He told me not to wash for a week. I was most annoyed when Mother made me wash before going to bed!

1938-Seriously Ill

In November 1938 I was taken ill with a very bad tummy. Dad rode down to the doctor's house at Swell, but Doctor Leslie King had gone hunting. On his return at about five o'clock he came to see me, still in his hunting clothes. I had a burst appendix. He got a taxi on his return to Swell and I was taken to Moreton Hospital to await a surgeon from Oxford, who was coming on the train to Moreton. I was unconscious and I was later told that Doctor King started the operation before the surgeon got there. He probably saved my life. I was six weeks in Moreton Hospital and did not go back to school until the following Easter.

The War

When war was declared in 1939 I was still going to Swell C.of E. School. Reg was at Northleach Grammar School. We had to carry gas masks to school and we had fire drill. We also stuck strips of sticky paper over the school windows to prevent the glass splintering in the event of being bombed. We needn't have bothered. The nearest bombs were fire bombs dropped at Upper Slaughter.

The Home Guard

In 1940 or 41 the Home Guard was formed. It was at first called the L.D.V. Local Defence Volunteers and later the Home Guard. Now Swell Hill was one of the highest places round Stow, so it was decided to site a lookout post there. Dad, having been in the 14-18 war, was most interested, and gave a lot of advice and enthusiasm. Our spare front room was handed over as a restroom, because each night four men reported for duty: two went straight to the lookout point, the other two slept on camp beds till after midnight. Then they went on duty while the other two got some sleep. Now and then the regular army, stationed at Maugersbury, would inspect them or call them out on manoeuvres. I remember one morning an army officer was driven into our yard about five o'clock. He woke Dad and also called the Home Guard out, saying it had been reported some German paratroops had landed near Guiting and they were to go with him in his truck. Dad, being an old soldier, lit the primus stove and made some tea, saying they would have to wait. He then called upstairs to Mother, "You'd better come down and cut some sandwiches. We don't know what time we shall be back". It turned out to be an exercise. I don't know if the officer knew it or not.

Another time the army and the Home Guard had a mock battle. The Home Guard had to defend Swell Hill while some men from the Guards Regiment had to get into the yard unseen by the defenders. An army major was in charge of the whole operation. As the exercise came to an end one man was missing, Dad. Search parties were sent out, the well was inspected- no sign of him anywhere. Then I noticed the bucket used for milking the house cow was missing. The major and myself crept to the cowshed door and peeped through a crack. Dad was milking the cow in his Home Guard uniform, forage cap turned sideways so it was ear to ear, softly singing to himself. When we opened the door he said there wasn't enough milk in the house for everyone to have a cup of tea, so he got a drop more. Talk about Dad's Army!

At about this time farmers were asked to push wagons and implements across roads to stop enemy vehicles in case of invasion. No one ever thought they might have come across the fields!

While the Home Guard had a post at Swell Hill an Airspeed Oxford training plane made a forced landing in a field next to our farm. It was in the dark and the Home Guard kept their distance, thinking it was an enemy plane. Eventually, one old home guard, Sandy Hall, said he would challenge them. He took his tunic off and approached them in shirt sleeves and carried no arms. He said "They will be less likely to shoot me if I'm a civilian". After a few days the wall to the next field was pulled down to make a longer runway and the plane flew back to Rissington. At about the same time two Fairy Battle aeroplanes crashed near Eyford Lakes, within two weeks of of one another, the air crews being killed on both occasions. I think there was an air pocket over the lakes causing the planes to suddenly lose height.

On the whole the war made very little difference to our way of life, as we always lived well, being mainly self sufficient. Dad killed two pigs most years. There were always several sides of bacon and hams hanging up in the kitchen. A lamb or two had to be killed because they had injured themselves mysteriously. We hunted with the gun; we had rabbit once or twice a week, pheasant, deer and partridge when in season. There was plenty of potatoes, as we were ordered by the government to grow a certain acreage. Dad was also a keen vegetable gardener and we also grew a field of roots for the sheep. We made sure that plenty of turnips and swedes were planted with the kale. My wage was 5 shillings (25p) a week and all the rabbits I could catch. I had started going to the pictures at Moreton-in-Marsh on Young's bus from Lower Swell, so I needed more money. I was getting 2/6 each for my rabbits,-two rabbits doubled my weekly wage. Some weeks I would sell ten or more. Reg joined the Fleet Air Arm and when he came home on leave we spent most of the time shooting or ferreting. He was a very good shot.

Northleach Grammar School

When Reg was eleven he passed to go to the grammar school at Northleach. Because we lived over a certain distance from the school bus route he was given a school bike, so Mum bought me one as well.

I hated school. I hated being shut indoors. I still do. All I could think about was open fields, cart horses and my little dog, which went everywhere with me. My parents later told me that I would lay down and go to sleep anywhere out of doors. They could always find me, as my little white dog would be sitting near me.

In 1941 I started at Northleach Grammar School, but I hated every minute of it. Reg did well at school. He left to join a firm of accountants at about the time I started. The teachers told me how clever my brother was and how thick I was. That didn't help!

I had to cycle the one and a half miles to catch the school bus, so it was quite easy to miss it. This I did about one day a week. Dad would greet me with "Missed the bus again! Get your old clothes on and meet me in the stable in five minutes". That made my day! Mother was not so understanding.

In the haymaking season of 1943 I was on top of a load of hay with Paddy, the man who had been working for Dad for several years, when the horses driven by Dad started off very quickly. I stuck my fork into the hay to save myself and stuck it straight through Paddy's foot. Dad said "That's it. You will have to do Paddy's work until he is better". I was over the moon! I never went back to school. My school report came by post and it read "I will not have him back at school unless his continued absence is explained". Dad said "That's alright. You don't want to go back do you?" Mother had other ideas!

Working as a boy-chap

So I never went to school after June 1944. I had to work hard but I loved every minute of it, mowing with two horses, hay turning with one horse in the "Martin's"side rake. The worst job was loading the wagon in front of the "Fennemore" hay loader, but Dad would stop the horses every twenty yards or so to give me time to arrange the hay on the wagon and get my feet out from underneath it. We had casual help come in the evenings and weekends so that helped me a lot. Paddy was back at work after about three weeks so I was demoted to under carter and under shepherd, under Dad. Our family had always been connected with sheep. There wasn't much else you could do on thin Cotswold soil before modern fertilisers. Without sheep to fertilise the land and muck from the cattle yards there would have been very poor crops. A field was always planted with roots, that is turnips, swedes and kale. The sheep were sometimes kept on the stubble after the corn was harvested and the swedes and turnips carried to them with a horse and cart, but generally the sheep were penned on the roots with hurdles or wire netting. You could tell by the following corn crop where they had been.

When I first left school I was known as a "boy-chap", that was really a boy who was working full time. My day comprised of getting up about seven. Dad was always up at six. He had boiled the kettle on the primus stove and lit the kitchen stove. By the time I came downstairs there was a cup of tea for me. I then went to the stable and put each horse a feed of corn and chaff in their mangers, then opened the horse ground gate. They usually came in on the trot. After I had tied them up I would untie the sheep dog. Then, depending on which field the sheep were in I would go and see them, either on my bike, on foot, or, if there was feed to take, with the horse and float.. While I was doing this Dad would milk the house cow and feed the calves and pigs with the surplus milk. Paddy, the carter, came at 7.30. He would give the horses a bit more feed, groom them, harness them and be out on the land with his team soon after eight o'clock.

Dad and myself went into breakfast about 8.30 or 9 o'clock. Breakfast was always fried home-cured bacon, with fried bread and eggs, sometimes with mushrooms or, in the summer, perhaps a tomato. After breakfast we usually had to give the sheep a pen, either on roots or grass seeds. This was one year later to be ploughed up for winter wheat in the autumn. After this I would have two horses to do whatever needed doing, perhaps some carting jobs, or perhaps land work, rolling, harrowing or suchlike.

Dinner was at 1o'clock, so that Dad could hear the one o'clock news on his battery radio while having his meal. Back to work at 2 until about 4. Then it was time to do the afternoon feeding.

Tea was about 5. Sometimes it was back to work in the summer, but in the winter we were back indoors trying to keep warm round the stove, with oil lamps for lighting. It was difficult to read, so about 8 o'clock I'd be in bed in the warm. Mum went about the same time. Dad liked to hear the headlines of the nine o'clock news. Of course there were exceptions. I would go to the Boys' Club at Swell one evening a week, and there was a whist drive once a fortnight which Mum and myself would attend. Dad would ride his old bike down to the "Golden Ball" on Saturday evenings, but be home about 9 o'clock. I went to the pictures at Moreton most weekends. When I was fifteen I joined the Young Farmer's Club at Moreton and Michael Oughton would take me in his father's Vauxhall car. Also, about this time I joined the Boxing Club at Moreton, so I was going out four or five nights a week. I also played football for Swell, so I had a busy social life.

Paddy the carter moved to another farm in 1946 and I worked the horses. My wage went up from 5 shillings to £1 per week. I spent most days walking behind a team of three horses wishing we had a tractor! Most of my friends in the Young Farmers' club drove tractors and used their fathers' cars, while I was still on a bike!

Dogs at Swell Hill

I would like to tell you about the dogs that I remember at Swell Hill. The first dog I remember, besides Mick the terrier, was Grandad's old English sheep dog called Bob. He lived in a kennel beside the drive and was tied to a very long chain which didn't quite reach across the drive. Now, if anyone walked straight down the drive Bob took little notice, but if they tried to creep past, out of his reach, he would bark and jump at them. If the chain had snapped I think he would have really savaged them. Us boys were told to keep away from him. When I was four I got in his kennel with him and we curled up in the straw together. My parents were scared for my safety. I think Bob growled at Dad when he got me out. Grandad sold Bob soon after and Dad bought a Welsh collie pup. He named him Towser. He was brown with white markings and was a useful sheep dog. Then, when I was about to leave school Dad bought me a border collie pup. It had a lot of white on it and I called him Jock. He was a lovely dog. When we left Swell Hill I gave him to one of my friends, Bob Lane, who had him for another eight or nine years.

Dad with a partridge & 'Mick'

All the time we had Towser and Jock we had a terrier as well. First it was Mick. Then we had Spot who would insist on going rabbiting on his own. One day he didn't come back. He was found some time later in Milton's well at Eyeford. Whether he fell in or the keeper had got fed up with him and shot him, putting him in the well, we never found out. Anyway after Spot Reg came home with a terrier cross whippet. This was the best ratter or rabbit dog I have ever known. He was brown and white, stood about sixteen inches high and had a lovely temperament. We called him Patch. He could outrun rabbits or smell them in holes in the ground or in holes in the old stone walls. I remember him "telling" at a hole in a wall and Reg putting his hand in from the other side. The dog grabbed his hand thinking it was the rabbit. It was a good job I was there to get the dog off. Reg had to go to the doctor's several days running to have the wound treated with a caustic pencil. There was no penicillin or antibiotics in those days.

There was a rubbish dump up the Cheltenham Road at The Beeches, about three quarters of a mile away. I used to go there with Patch on Sunday mornings ratting. An old chap named Jack lived in a hut on the site. I think the council paid him to level the rubbish and keep the site tidy. He would always have something to sell such as bicycle wheels and boards. Well, once I'd taken Patch there he would go on his own. When I went to collect him Jack would have him in his hut sitting by the fire. As soon as we got Patch home he was back there again! So in the end we gave him to Jack who thought the world of him. He had him for several years and I bet he kept Jack in rabbit stew!

After Patch we had another Jack Russell type terrier named Spot. It was a bitch this time and she never went off. We still had her when we left Swell and took her with us. I've always had bitches since. They stay at home better.

Pig Killing

Dad had learnt the butchering trade when he was a young man, so killing the pigs for the house twice a year was no problem. He usually killed one pig about October and another in February. We had to do it in cold weather or the meat wouldn't keep. The pig usually weghed about fifteen score, that's three hundred pounds. It would not be fed the last twenty four hours, only given water to drink. Plenty of hot water and clean dry straw were got ready. The pig was led out on a cord and Dad would stick it. There was no law about using a gun in those days. I think the pig killers were more skilled. The knife touched the heart and it was all over. The carcass was wiped with a cloth and warm water to remove any blood. You see water will dry but blood doesn't. The pig was then laid on clean straw, belly down. Some more straw was loosely shaken on top, then set on fire to burn the bristles off. The pig was then turned over and the process repeated. When all the bristles were burnt off the pig was washed to remove the black. It was then hung up from a beam by its back legs and the chitterlings removed, together with the liver and lights and the veil which you wrapped the faggots in. If we had killed the pig say at ten in the morning, we would have liver for dinner at one o'clock. If you have never had fresh liver you've never lived!

The pig was left to hang about forty eight hours. Then it was lowered onto a bench and cut up. The hams and sides were put into the salting lead, but the ribs were removed together with any other pig meat from the inside of the pig. These were shared with the neighbours, to be roasted fresh. The neighbours returned the compliment when they killed their pigs. The head was made into brawn. The chitterlings were thoroughly cleaned and put into salt water. They were turned daily for five days, then boiled. You could then eat them cold or fry them. They were delicious.

Lambs' Tails

Another delicacy was lambs' tails. The lambs' tails were not removed until we had finished lambing, so some of the early ones were quite big. One man held the lamb sitting on a board and another man cut the tail off quickly with a red hot iron. The lamb did not seem at all distressed. It was done quickly and properly. (The R.S.P.C.A. have rightly or wrongly stopped this practice. The lamb now has a rubber ring placed on its tail. It lies down and wriggles about for five minutes or so and it takes about two weeks for the tail to drop off).

Anyway, when we burnt them off we had a pot of water boiling on a wood fire nearby. As soon as a tail was cut us boys had a loop of string on it and held it in the boiling water for about one minute. Then all the wool came off it. Some people made lambs tail pie. We liked the tails fried in egg and breadcrumbs. I wish I had some now!

Goodbye to Swell Hill

Swell Hill was owned by Grandad's brother William, who lived in South Africa. He came over to see Dad and the farm in the spring of 1939. The Cotswold slate roofs on the house and buildings were in bad repair, and there was no water supply, only rainwater caught in underground tanks. Well, with the roofs in bad repair we were not catching much rain! Uncle Will decided to have the roofs repaired and the mains water put on, either from Swell or Condicote, so we could milk cows which was the most profitable thing at the time. Well, before the work could start, Uncle was told by the shipping line that if he didn't go back to Africa immediately they couldn't guarantee him a passage because it looked as if war was breaking out with Germany and all civilian shipping would cease until after hostilities. Uncle said "The war wont last long. Do what you can to keep the farm together and I'll be back in a year or so!".

Dad got the local builder, Cox Howman, to do the house roof and put in some new window frames. He also put a new main beam in the bottom barn, and did several other urgent repairs. He also bought some new gates, which in his agreement were the landlord's responsibility. He expected to be repaid in a year or two when the war ended.

The war went on for six years. Uncle Will died. The farm was left to his son, Bill, who never replied to Dad's letters or solicitors' letters. Finally, a letter came to say Bill was selling the farm by auction. Dad was heartbroken. No way could he buy the farm as he had spent most of his money on doing it up.

Dad's sister came from New Zealand in 1947. She tried to contact young Bill in South Africa, but he didn't want to know. Aunt Mabel thought the best thing would be for us to emigrate to New Zealand. So Dad gave in his notice to quit the farm in September 1948. Our passage to New Zealand was booked for October 1948 and our farm dispersal sale was to be in September. Then disaster struck. In May Dad was taken ill and rushed to Cheltenham Hospital where he died after two weeks. My brother, Reg, his wife, Mavis, and children, John and Jane, eventually did go to New Zealand. But Mum and myself decided to stay in the Cotswolds.

Although I hear from branches of the Stayt Family from all over the world no-one ever mentions Bill in South Africa!

1947 Swell Hill. Me, Dad, Norman Izod, Reg Hunt & my brother Reg

Last Days at Swell Hill

The farm was bought by an old bachelor. The sale was to be completed by 29th September, when we had to vacate. Meanwhile, we allowed the bachelor to live in part of the house.

I was not quite eighteen and fit and there was a lot to do. The house cow had to be milked and calves fed with the surplus milk from the day before. Then there were about 230 ewes with their lambs. They were penned in wire netting and had the pen extended every day, and I had to watch them for maggots. Then I would fetch the horses in and give them a feed. Soon after Dad's death I started mowing the hay with two horses pulling the Bartlett mower. I worked a pair of horses for about two hours and then let them rest and feed from a pile of cut grass while another pair did their two hours. Doing it this way I could cut about an acre an hour. When the grass was dry on top I turned it, with one horse pulling the Martin's Swathe Turner. Then I realised what kind neighbours we had. One lent me a tractor and hay sweep and an elevator, and another a man to help. We swept about 15 acres of hay to the corner of the field and made two large ricks. Mum and Reg's wife, Mavis, helped put it in the elevator and luckily the weather was good. As soon as we had finished the hay the corn was ready, about 120 acres of it. We hired a neighbour and his Combine. The sacks of corn were dropped around the field as they were filled, so it was quite a heavy job collecting them. Once again another neighbour came to the rescue, lending a tractor and trailer and a man to help.

Asthalleigh, near Minster Lovell

All this time I was looking for a job with a house for Mum and myself as well as getting ready for the sale. I went to see several jobs and in the end chose a farmer near Minster Lovell. He didn't show us the cottage as he said someone was in it and he didn't want them to know they were getting the sack. He promised the earth, said he had known Dad and he wanted me to be his assistant. Well, we moved the day after our farm sale. When we got there we had a shock. The cottage was falling down, but the farmer promised to do it up immediately.

We started milking at 5 o'clock in the morning. The boss had already got the cows in and had started milking. There were five of us and we milked about 50 cows, by hand. We were home to breakfast about 7. Then our day jobs started at 7.30. Two of the farmer's men had been working there for about 25 years. They took no notice of the boss at all. They were both very skilled and knew what wanted doing, and got on with it. This annoyed the boss who was a little man with a temper. They just ignored him and didn't answer him if he was in a mood. The rest of the staff was a man who did the retail milk round, a land girl and a displaced person. The only good things about the farmer was he paid a bit more than the going rate and he liked you to be home by a quarter to five.

The family in the cottage next door were very kind to us. There were three sons and a daughter. Two sons were married but the eldest son lived at home and was one of the ones who had worked on the farm for 25 years. The daughter was Mary, who is now my wife. So, although moving there was a disaster, some good came of it!

Bledington

I only stayed near Minster Lovell six months. We moved to Bledington where I looked after the arable on a small estate. I had sole charge of a tractor and also a horse for the lighter jobs. He was a Suffolk called Prince. That's when I realised that I missed the horses. Well, everything was going fine. I would see Mary two or three times a week and I enjoyed the work. There was also a good football team at Bledington and I was playing regularly. Then my boss inherited a very large estate in Hampshire on his father's death, so he moved, asking me if I would like to go with him. But I declined because of Mary and the many friends I had in this area. So he recommended me to his friend at Westcote, Captain Millais, where I have been ever since.

Part 2
Westcote

I started work at Westcote Manor on May 1st 1950, looking after some grazing cattle and about 20 acres of arable, about half of which grew potatoes from seed for a Dutch firm called Veribest. These were picked by hand, employing local women. I filled my time in the gardens, which were kept immaculate by Arthur Rowland, the gardener and Mrs. Millais and sometimes casual help. The gardens were open to the public on several occasions in aid of various charities. Captain Raoul Millais is a professional artist and neither he nor Mrs. Millais interfered with what I did on the farm, or what Mr. Rowland did in the gardens. It was a happy workplace and we all got on well together.

When we moved to Manor Cottage it was in a state of bad repair, but the Millais had builders in straight away and put a Rayburn cooker in the kitchen and made a bathroom. Hot water out of taps was a luxury for us! Although I was out quite a bit I think Mum was happy. We had a good next door neighbour, Gladys, who came in regularly to see if we needed anything. There were whist drives occasionally in the village hall and also at Gawcombe, which Mum liked to attend.

Making Ends Meet

The farm wage was £4. 15 shillings a week, that is £4. 75 p now. But how much further the money went! I would give my mother my wage packet and she gave me 5 shillings, (25p). I would get more money by catching rabbits, sweeping chimneys and working for other people at weekends. I did quite a bit of dry stone walling around Stow and Broadwell and, although I hate the job, I did some decorating.

After I had been at Westcote two years Mr. Will Simms offered to sell me a piece of land, about half an acre up on what is known as Westcote Hill. He had bought it some years before from four different people. He still had the receipts, which I now have in the bank. I think I gave him £25 for it , over 5 week's wages, which is about the same value as it would be now. Owning this land enabled me to buy stock of my own. I put a shed up and fenced it in. Then I started dealing in my spare time. I have dealt in goats, sheep, pigs cows, horses donkeys and poultry.

I also dealt in second hand cars and lorries. I started collecting scrap from local farms and farm sales. When I had two or three tons I would get someone to take it to Swindon for me. The scrap iron never made much profit, but if I could find some lead, copper or brass in amongst it that was always good money. I have known copper or brass around £100 per cwt. I had quite a lot of scrap cars when the R.A.F. left Little Rissington Aerodrome, which I cut up for scrap. Then the authorities got on to me saying I needed a license to have a scrap yard. So I packed that up.

I then bought 12 donkeys which I hired out at weekends for donkey racing at fetes etc. In the meantime I had bought another field from Mr. George Townsend of Fifield. This is a steep bank of about two acres, not far from my other field. This had no fence around it, so after fencing it I put the donkeys in there and fed them hay on top of the thorn bushes that were in the middle of the field. Well, in two years the thorns disappeared with the donkeys continually biting them. However, when I took the donkeys away the thorns came thicker than ever. In fact over half the field is covered with thorns now.

These fields are quite isolated and over the years I have had a lot of things stolen, from a goat to bales of hay, bags of animal feed, my gas cutting gear, a large bench vice and very nearly three young horses. I had bought three chestnut fillies from beside the road at Stow Fair and put them in the half acre paddock with some feed. I went and saw them last thing at night and they were lying down quite happy. First thing the next morning they were missing. Someone had been there in the night and made an alley with oil drums and car doors and anything else they could find. Then they backed a lorry to the end of the alley -you could see the wheel marks, and I thought they had loaded the horses and gone. The police came out and confirmed everything I suspected. I kept thinking these three unbroken fillies would be difficult to load in the dark. Then we thought we could trace where they had jumped the barricades, but we weren't sure. Later in the day the game keeper from Barrington came to say there were three horses the other side of the airfield. Was I pleased! Had they been quieter I would certainly have lost them!

All the time I worked for Captain Millais I never asked for any overtime or bonus. He allowed me to use his tractor whenever I wanted and also to keep animals of my own on the farm. This arrangement suited me better. Several years running I bought an unbroken pony at Stow Fair, broke it in and then sold it on at a little profit. Anything it made over cost was profit as it cost me nothing to keep. My mentor was an elderly gentleman named Cecil Scarrott who lived at Broadwell. He was a real dealer. He didn't drive, so if you wanted to sell him something you had to fetch him to see it. If you sold him something you had to deliver it. If you bought something from him you had to collect it. So anything he sold at a profit was all profit as he had no expenses. He was also a great man for swapping things and drawing a bit of money as well. If you think about it you could live this way.

The Railway Closures of the Fifties

After Dr. Beeching closed the small railway stations in the fifties I was in a chip shop in Stow and got talking to three men who were employed by Baileys, the big scrap firm from Cheltenham. They were removing the railway lines between Kingham and Bourton-on-the-Water. They asked me if I knew anyone who would buy all the sleepers. They had sold a few to the neighbouring farms but there were between twelve and fifteen hundred left. I asked the price and was told 2/6 each, that's about twelve and a half pence. I had to take the lot. Some were nearly new and some were rotten. I think we settled for £140. I agreed to have them. I came home and got the money. It was Saturday lunchtime and I went with another man and we had the first load home that afternoon. We fetched two more loads on the Sunday. Then I started selling them for whatever I could get. We stacked the sound ones for resale and sawed the rotten ones for firewood. For the next two or three weeks I took sandwiches and a thermos for lunch. I would borrow the tractor from the Manor, go and put 20 sleepers on the trailer, then eat my lunch while driving home. After the first week I wished I had never bought them! Then I had a bit of luck. A farmer from near Moreton came to buy some from me. I sold him 250 of the ones still on the line at 10/- each so I didn't have to handle them. When the scrap men had finished and I had collected all the sleepers I drove the tractor and trailer the length of the line from Bourton to Kingham with four or five boys picking up the iron nuts which had been cut off the chairs which held the lines. These amounted to more than a ton and came to over £30, so I ended up alright, but it was a lot of hard work!

Farming in Westcote

When I came to Westcote in 1950 there were two farms, two market gardens and three smallholdings in Church Westcote, and four farms in Nether Westcote. About half the men in the two Westcotes were employed on the land one way or another. There were still about ten carthorses working in the two villages. Mr. Bill Simmonds, who farmed and was also the village carpenter and undertaker, used only horses on his farm. Although he had quite a small farm he employed three men. John Hunt worked the horses and also helped milk the cows with his brother, Fred, who still lives in the village. What a lovely sight it was on a frosty morning to see John Hunt ploughing! His horses always looked fat and well. They pulled together quite effortlessly and all you could hear was the clink of chains and the squeak of leather. Bill Simmonds' brother, Ernest, farmed just across the road. He kept good beef cattle and had quite a lot of arable. He employed two men. One was Bert Durham who drove the tractor. The other was Mr. Simmonds' brother Chris, who looked after the cattle and loved to work the horse doing carting jobs and light land work such as harrowing and hay-turning.

The Simmonds' farms were in Nether Westcote. There were two other farms there. One was Manor Farm which was just below Ernie Simmonds. This farm changed hands four times in as many years at just about the time I came to Westcote. The last people to buy were the Scaramangers who stayed nearly forty years. The other farm was owned by the Gibsons who were the biggest landowners and owned two other sets of farm buildings as well as Field Farm where they lived. One son, John, ran a taxi as well as working on the farm. John had two sons, Tony and Paul. Tony now runs the "Cotswold Guesthouse", which stands on the site of one of their farms. The old Gibson Family employed several men. They milked a small herd of cows, had some beef cattle and grew corn. Although they had a tractor they still worked a pair of carthorses.

At Church Westcote Stayt's Farm was farmed by Mr. Esau Griffin and his two sons, Jim and John. They milked cows, supplying some of the houses in the village, the rest going to the dairy who collected the churns every morning from the roadside. They used two carthorses to do the work, until the year before they sold up when they bought a Fordson tractor. John drove it but the brothers were not mechanically minded so it stood in the barn most of the time!

The other Church Westcote Farm was The Manor where I worked.

There were also two market gardeners who both specialised in strawberries which could be grown out of season. One was Mr. Tozer and the other was Mr. Brain. Both employed women from the village and during the busy season quite a few pickers from the local R.A.F. Station at Little Rissington.

The three smallholdings were run by Mr. Charlie Clews, who worked on the aerodrome, Mr. Will Simms who was of retirement age and Mr. Arthur Gibson, who ran the largest with his son, Bill. Besides doing their own work Arthur and Bill worked on other farms, helping with the haymaking, harvesting and threshing. Bill had a Fordson tractor to do the land work, which he later exchanged for a small Ferguson which was much handier. He also had a small corn mill with which he ground corn for other people.

When I came to Westcote nearly every householder had a few chickens in the garden and I should think one in five had a pig to be fattened and killed. I think almost everyone had a good vegetable garden and a lot of potatoes were grown. The men who worked on the farms were often allowed to grow potatoes in the field beside their bosses'. This left more room in their gardens for the greenstuff. Nothing was wasted. It was fed to the pig or the neighbouring pig if you hadn't got one. The farmers all grew what were referred to as roots. If you were a dairy farmer you would grow kale, perhaps some turnips or swedes and almost certainly mangolds. The sheep men would grow more swedes and turnips and some kale. So the farmer you did a few jobs for or were friendly with would always let you get a few turnips or swedes. These were probably the main vegetables for Sunday dinner.

A lot of the women went wooding, collecting any fallen sticks and taking them home for the winter. I have seen five or six prams and trucks returning from Gawcombe Wood overladen with wood and the women all talking and laughing. I think it was quite a social occasion!

Gawcombe

The largest farm in the parish is Gawcombe. When I came to Westcote it was owned by a Mr. Wagner. He employed some fifteen to twenty people on the farm and in the gardens. They milked a herd of Red Poll cattle and kept a large flock of Southdown sheep. The whole place was very tidy. The hedges were kept cut and ditches dug. Gates all swung. It was really a pleasure to see. They also had a room in one of the farm buildings where they held parties , whist drives, film shows etc. and the village people were welcome to attend.

When the Wagners moved away Colonel Stud bought the estate and it was run much the same way. Colonel and Mrs. Stud were very nice people. They still let the women go wooding and had a kind word for everyone. Both the Colonel and Mrs. Stud were keen foxhunters. They had very good horses which they also raced. But farming was not so profitable in the late fifties so they couldn't employ quite so much labour. I think the Colonel was not in the best of health and they gave up the estate in the early sixties and moved to a smaller place at Slaughter.

The new owner had modern ideas and bought more land and modern machines. He grubbed a lot of the hedges out to make the fields larger. There was a grant paid towards this work. The land was nearly all arable and had grown some good crops. Now, the estate was no longer run in a friendly family way but as a commercial unit. Then the government scheme was brought in to stop over-production of grain and the whole of Gawcombe was taken out of farming and allowed to grow wild. It's what is known as "set aside". Owners are paid a lot by the Common Market not to farm their land, when half the world is starving. I have just been told that the government are going to pay out again. This time to replant the hedges! I don't think this is the way to look after the countryside.

Westcote in 1950

Before I moved to Westcote I had been through the village on a number of occasions and noticed there were still small strips of land which were left over from the Middle Ages and the Feudal System and always thought perhaps the place was a bit behind the times. I think it was, and still is, I'm glad to say. The mains water was laid on about the time I came. Until then people fetched their water either from a well or from a spring. There must be at least ten wells in the two Westcotes and several springs. As soon as the mains water was laid on the Water Board said the well and spring water was unfit to drink and condemned it. Westcote inhabitants had drunk nothing else for hundreds of years! You could still see the old men of the village using a yoke to carry water from the pump to their livestock, or to water the allotments. Many men still cut grass on the sides of the road to give to their horse or pig or make into hay for the winter.

What I noticed more than anything else was the friendliness of everyone. If you went up the road any time of day you would meet someone to chat with. I mentioned this to one old man. He replied "We ain't friendly, just nosy!"

Householders in Westcote
Church Westcote

In 1950 there were about twenty four houses in Church Westcote and eighteen in Nether Westcote. We will start with the Manor in Church Westcote. This house was bought by Captain and Mrs. Millais in 1948 and they moved in 1949. The Dower House next door belonged to the Long Family. They had lived there a long time and also owned the Dower House cottage. Opposite the Dower House cottage is Church Cottage. This was originally a service cottage belonging to Gawcombe Estate, but it had been bought by Jim Griffin and he lived there with his wife and two children, Anne and James. Just above Church Cottage was "the Guggle", which shared the same path and looked out onto the same open plan garden. Don and Audrey Coombes lived there and later bought Close Cottage, where they lived until they took over the pub.

Next to "The Guggle" was a cottage facing the road. This was the home of Mr. and Mrs. Arthur Gibson and their son, Bill. Round the corner was Mr. and Mrs. Charlie Clews' cottage, which also served as the Post Office, Mrs. Clews being the postmistress. The other cottage next to them was occupied by their eldest son and his wife, Bernard and Nancy Clews.

The blue slated cottage, facing the road, was lived in by Mr. and Mrs. Fred Newman. Fred was one of the oldest men in the village and at one time owned a horse and cart, which he hired out to the council, besides taking and fetching to Stow Station for Westcote people. Next door to the Newmans was "Close Cottage", where Mr. and Mrs. Tucker lived. I think they were Londoners who moved here during the war. "The Close" itself was occupied by a couple named Freeman who were townspeople and complained about nearly everything that happened in the village! Next door to them was "Stayt's Farm", where Mr. Esau Griffin lived with his son, John.

Then there was the top end of the village. St. John's Cottage was occupied by Mrs. Roberts and her two daughters, Margaret and Celia. Next came four council houses which were just completed. Numbers 1 and 2 were never built. They started at number 3, which was occupied by Mr. and Mrs. Connolly, their son, Ted, and Mrs. Connolly's father "Pop" Clayton. They came from London and were very popular in the village. Pop's tales of when he was a "totter" in London were hilarious.

Number 4 was occupied by the Robinsons and their four boys and one girl. Mr. Robinson, "Darkie", worked on the building, but was a wonderful mechanic. He spent any spare time he had repairing local peoples' cars, motor bikes, bicycles, lawn mowers and anything else. He did all this for very little reward and a lot of the children would not have had bikes but for Darkie. He was a lovely person who had time for everyone. He sadly passed away recently. Number 5 was the home of Alf and Nancy Burdock with two sons, David and Keith and twin daughters, Christine and Veronica. Number 6 was home to an elderly couple, George and Lily Newman- I think cousins of Fred Newman.

Along the top road, above what was then the school, are four more council houses. Going from the end nearest Nether Westcote, there lived Will Simms, with two sons, Arthur and Walter and daughter, Emily. Next to them were the Hunts, Jack and Mrs. Hunt, and, I think, eight children. Next again, was Harry Burdock, his wife, two sons and two daughters.

Then came The Convent, with its 12 or 14 Anglican nuns.

One more house, on the corner of Field Road, was "Four Winds", where a Miss Elliott and her companion lived.

I moved to Manor Cottages. The cottage I lived in was previously occupied by Alf Burdock. Gladys St Roas lived in the other one, with her daughters, Maxine and Maurita.

In the Manor farmyard was a bungalow, converted from a cartshed. This is where Arthur Rowland, the Manor gardener lived. The only other two houses had the market gardens of Mr. Tozer and Mr. Brain.

I've been all round the village and nearly forgot one of the most important houses, The Rectory. Reverend Walmsley was rector here when I came. Reverend Stanley Bubb came about two years later. He was the vicar at Lower Slaughter before that.

Nether Westcote

In Nether Westcote there were two houses only on the right hand side of the road, coming from Church Westcote. The first one, next to the quarry, was "Far Furlong". Mrs. Worgan lived there with her two daughters, Vi and Mary. I think Mrs. Worgan was the schoolteacher at Westcote and I think Vi took over when she retired. Next door was the home of Stan and Hilda Davis. Stan was a carpenter and cabinet maker by trade. His wife was Mr. and Mrs. Tucker's daughter from "Close Cottage". There was one bungalow on the bottom side of the road where Howard Griffin lived alone.

Honeysuckle Cottage, on the corner, was two cottages. Mrs. Howard lived in one. She was sister to Alf and Harry Burdock. Next door is the Chapel. The only house below the Chapel was Pitts Farm, where Bill Simmonds lived and farmed.

On the other side of the road, at the top, is Well House. This is where Mr. and Mrs. George Ward lived.

"Buena Vista", the cottage facing northeast, was home to Mr. and Mrs. Chris Simmonds who were a lovely couple very quiet and reserved, but when you called on them they made you most welcome. Mr. Simmons would cut mens' hair for a few pence he cut mine many times.

Just below was another farm, belonging to Mr. Ernest Simmonds. They kept beef cattle and grew corn. Mrs. Simmonds also kept quite a lot of poultry. Right next door was Manor Farm. The owners, the Freemans, moved out about the time I came to Westcote and the Scaramangers bought it.

The cottage just below Manor Farm ,on the corner, was occupied by Mr. Simmonds and Mrs Dolly Simmonds. Just round the corner from that was Bill Simmonds' carpenter's shop. Behind that was Len Durham's home. Then there was a pair of cottages called "Pencross". One was the home of Mrs. Mabel Davis, whose husband had farmed Manor Farm some years before. The other was empty.

Of course, the pub was opposite the carpenter's shop. On the Church Westcote side of this is a cottage which was owned by Mrs. Large, who had a son, Michael and a daughter, Mary. The small cottage the other side was the home of George Haynes.

The only other dwellings in Nether Westcote were Field Farm, the home of the Gibson family, who owned most of the land around Westcote. Opposite Field Farm was Virginia Cottage, where I think Stan Gibson lived before moving to Stow.

"The New Inn"

I suppose the centre of the village was the New Inn, with, I suppose, eight or ten regulars and about as many casuals, except for the weekends when the pub was usually full, a lot of them wives who came to keep an eye on their menfolk!

In 1950 best bitter was 1/- (five p) a pint, mild was 11d (four and a half p), cider 9d (three and a half p). Mr. Walter Coombes was landlord. I don't know how many years he had been there. When he retired his son, Don, took over for another thirty odd years.

There were some real characters using the pub in my early days, like Charlie Card and his son, Bill. They lived in an old cottage down in Bill Simmond's fields. They had no water or electricity, no road of any sort and were half a mile from the village. They visited the pub every evening. Charlie had an enormous moustache. There were often bets placed as to how long it was. I saw it measured once. I think it was eleven and a half inches. Bill had lost a leg in the war and had an artificial leg or was sometimes on crutches. They could both drink enormous amounts of cider and were good company. When the pub shut at 10pm you could see their outline wandering down the fields, with a hurricane lamp swinging between them.

Another cider drinker was Jack Hunt, father of a large family. He was a very hard worker who would help anyone and give anybody anything, but, as soon as he had a few extra bob he'd have a day on the drink. He used to say, "It's my money and I've spent it". On several occasions he said to me" It doesn't matter if you haven't got any money as long as you don't owe any". When Jack had had a few pints he would sing the old songs, and we would join in the choruses. Alas, a lot of these songs are forgotten now. Some of his family still live in the area. One son, Fred, lives in the village. He is a hard worker who can turn his hand to anything, and like his dad is kind and forthright, and he likes a drop of cider! Jack would be proud of him.

Chapel Goers

Now, besides the regulars at the pub, there were about six elderly men, who were, I think, strict chapel. They didn't use the pub, but they were very interesting to talk to. Three or four of these could often be found having a good old chinwag in the road. Although they had the same thoughts on religion they didn't agree on much else, especially politics! If you were allowed to join their little circle and turned the subject to politics you could walk away and they'd still be arguing an hour later, with much waving of arms and stamping of feet. Billy Simmonds was usually to the forefront of these gatherings. When the present Queen was crowned a public holiday was declared. We had a party in the Tithe Barn, now the Village Hall. The organisers didn't know quite how the chapel goers and the Brethren would react to the large amounts of beer and cider which we provided, so we seated them all at one end of the room. We need not have worried. I was one of the people going round with a cider jug, and they drunk as much as anyone else. As someone remarked later it didn't seem to affect them. Perhaps they were used to it!

Tattle

Tattle always grew an early bite of grass, and the locals with animals would mind them there in the spring. I can remember the Griffins trying to finish milking a bit earlier in the morning so as to graze their cows before the Hunt lads came home to breakfast, bringing Billy Simmonds' cows with them. It almost got to blows at times over the grass on the common. Before I came to Westcote Mr. Walter Coombes who kept the New Inn had five or six milking cows. Also, he sold milk around the village and grazed on Tattle. Then there were the owners of working horses who would graze mostly in the evenings and water the horses at the same time at the lovely spring there.

Fred Hunt used to keep about twenty ducks on Tattle, shutting them up at night in a wooden hut he made. The ducks thrived. They laid well and kept the weeds down around the spring. It's all overgrown now. There was quite a large disused quarry at the Nether Westcote end where people could dump their rubbish.

Most summer evenings children could be seen and heard playing on the Church Westcote end, cricket, rounders and other games, often with some grown-ups joining them. I don't remember anyone complaining about the mess the cows and horses made!

The footpath across Tattle was well worn. It was the short cut to the pub, not only for the folk from Church Westcote, but also for those from Gawcombe and from R.A.F. Little Rissington. Besides the airmen there were always builders who lived on the camp all week, going home at weekends.

Gypsies have used Tattle as an occasional stopping place, especially at Stow Fair times. I have been told a family camped there during the war, with the children going to Westcote School and the men working on local farms. There are not many of the old Romany Gypsies travelling the roads now. A lot of them have bought houses and smallholdings and settled down. Many of the travellers are not gypsies at all. Some have just tried to get out of the rat race, but I'm afraid some are wasters who have been kicked out of council houses, or have been in trouble with the Law and are trying to lose themselves.

Newcomers to Westcote

When people move into this village they nearly all say what a beautiful village it is and how lucky they are to have found it. When they tell me how much they like everything to do with Westcote I often say, "I bet you will want to change something before long". I remember one lady answering, "Oh no I wont. It's perfect". Within a week she says to me "Who gave those horrible people permission to park their caravans on the green?", referring to the gypsies who have been coming for hundreds of years and whom most of the villagers are on first name terms with.

We had another lady who bought a house opposite the Village Hall. She first phoned the police because Jack Hunt's cockerel was crowing at 6 o'clock in the morning! Then she called the police out because she could hear the music when there was a party in the Village Hall. The funny thing was a police sergeant and constable came into the Hall, had a drink and a sandwich and said the music couldn't be heard twenty yards away and to carry on. The next day the lady said to me "I don't think much of your police. I phoned them them last night and they never came out". She moved just after!

I am not against newcomers. In fact some of my best friends have moved in recent years. What I cant understand is why, as soon as some people move in they acquire two dogs, usually large ones. Now, legally they have nowhere to exercise these dogs as it's an offence for a dog to mess on the highway or any public place, and certainly an offence to take a dog onto someone else's property without their permission. A farming friend, not too far from Oxford, asked a man who was walking on a footpath across her field, to put his dog on a lead. This he refused to do. Well, one thing led to another and it ended in the High Court. The judge ruled that footpaths across private lands were for people, not dogs, and she had every right to stop people from bringing dogs unleashed.

Some people moved in about three years ago who had a dog which was always roaming the village. I warned them a couple of times that he'd come to a sticky end if I caught him in our lambing pen again. They didn't seem able to keep him at home, or didn't bother to try. He was here at 7 o'clock one morning and I shut him up in a stable. Nobody looked for him, so before I sent him home I rubbed him all over with blood from a deer which had been run over on the road. I watched the dog go to their door and bark. Well, they came to the door. I was out in the road. It was dark so they couldn't see me. "Do you think he's been hit by a car?" says the woman to her husband. "Can't see any marks on him", says the husband. "I hope he hasn't been killing sheep" one of them said. I met this couple in the road a few days later. After passing the time of day I said "By the way, where was your dog last Saturday?" They both said together "Oh he never went out of the house all day!" These are quite wealthy business people who probably think they are one above us country folk. They are not!

Nearly everyone agrees that the houses and cottages in the Cotswolds are some of the nicest in the country. Do we ever stop to think that when they were built, perhaps two or three hundred years ago, there was no planning authority? The people who paid for the building used their common sense. Local stone was quarried close to the site. Most of the timber was cut nearby. Any boards or planks for floors etc were sawn in the saw pit at the local carpenter's. The houses were built by local tradesmen who would be seeing their work for the rest of their lives, and the owner of the building would be rewarded with something very long-lasting and pleasing to the eye, not because he could sell it at a profit and move on somewhere else. I can just remember before and during the war when a house changed hands the new occupier would perhaps have it painted and a few slates put on the roof, then live in it for some time before he did any alterations- I suppose to get a feeling for it. Now, when a cottage or house changes hands the first thing the new owner does, before he moves in, is to knock two rooms into one, or build something on, or take something off. He usually stays two or three years, then the next owner puts it back to how it was originally and so it goes on!

I don't understand why we judge other people whom we have never met. I find this a lot with people who want to part with an animal, especially horses and dogs. How often have I heard "I ought to get rid of my horse as I can't afford to feed it properly and I haven't time to exercise it, but I'm frightened it might go to a bad home!" I have sold many horses and have followed a lot of them up. These have all got better lives than they had with me. In my experience good animals get good homes, yet a lot of people think they are better than anyone else. You notice the proper gypsy horses are always fat and healthy because they are their investments, their bank. They don't want anything to happen to them.

About three years ago two ladies knocked on our door. I recognised one of them as someone who had just moved to the village a week before. They were in their new green wellies and Barbour coats and each carried a new basket with a kitchen knife resting in the bottom. "We were told that you would know where the mushrooms grow", said one. Now what made them think I was going to tell them? I knew where some mushrooms grew. Most people who have lived here long have their own secret patch in a field somewhere, but you certainly don't tell anyone else! I found out later that some wag had set them up by telling them to get big baskets and come and see me!

Another thing happened about the same time. A lady said to me that she remembered when she was young going into the country and picking wild violets, but she didn't think there were any left now. I took her about twenty yards from where we were talking and showed her a patch of violets growing under a wall. She was overjoyed and immediately started picking. I suggested she didn't pick too many and older people just picked enough to go in an eggcup. Later that day I saw two girls, about 12 or 14, picking. I went and had a word with them. They said "Our auntie said we could pick them. We are going to take them home to London with us". They picked every one and I don't think there's been any there since!

Old Country Pastimes

I remember, from about 1935, it seemed that even games and pastimes had their seasons and you never heard children say that they were bored! Most children had little jobs to do after school and before they were allowed to play. A lot of cottages still had no piped water, so, as soon as you were big enough, you helped fetch the water in buckets from a tap in the street or from the brook. Another little job was to get the morning wood. There was no central heating and all the stoves and kitchen ranges went out at night and had to be relit in the early morning to boil the kettle. Then there was the allotment. There was always something to do there, if only to fetch the vegetables for the next day. The other thing was running errands. As there were very few telephones or cars the children were the main source of communication. It was nothing for children of 10 or 11 to walk three miles with a letter, or perhaps a small gift for someone. You were usually timed on these journeys, and God help you if you were too long!

Rag rugs

Many of the women made rag rugs in the winter evenings. They got a piece of clean sacking and a wooden peg, a little larger than a pencil and any material to hand. The material was cut into strips two inches wide and about six inches long. A hole was made in the sackcloth with the peg, the strip of material passed through, then back through another hole close by and tied in a knot. This was repeated all over the sacking. By using different coloured rags some lovely patterns were made. To complete the job the rug would be laid on the floor and clipped with scissors to make a nice finish. These rugs were very warm, hard wearing and cost nothing to make. Whole families would sit round the fire "rugging" on a winter's evening, perhaps enjoying a drop of hot cider or home-made wine. Remember there was no T.V. and nearly all the radios were battery operated so you only had them on occasionally, or the battery ran flat.

Childrens' Games

One of the favourite games on a summer's evening was "Fox and Hounds". One was chosen to be the fox and he or she would run off. As soon as he was out of sight the rest would set off after him, making a noise like a pack of hounds. When the fox was lost from view, one of the hounds would call "Holler or the hounds wont follow!" The fox would then call out and away the whole lot would go again. They must have run several miles some evenings. What good healthy fun it was. As the parents were nearly all connected with farming in some way, the children had been taught from an early age that you never walked in a crop, whether it was corn or hay, or in anything else that could be harvested. If you climbed over a gate you did so at the hinge end, otherwise you made the gate drag. You never ran through a flock of sheep and you never made holes in fences.

All the games seemed to have seasons. As the ground started to dry in the spring out came the marbles! The old lady who kept the village shop knew just when to put a few in the window. That would get the children going, spending their halfpennies and pennies.

The first of May was Maypole Day. The children would get into little gangs and collect wild flowers and tie them to broom handles or sticks of some kind. Then they would go round the houses like carol singers do, showing off their garlands of flowers and singing

"All around the maypole, trit trit trot
See what a maypole we have got
Buttercups and daisies and all the pretty flowers
That come in the Spring to join our sunny hours".

Then one child would knock on the door and hope to get a copper or two.

About the same time of year the hoops would come out. Some were wooden hoops, but a lot were made out of iron. A few of these were made by the blacksmith, but many were the tyres from the old root drills, where the wooden spokes had rotted away and the rims were of no use to the farmer. You ran with your hoop as fast as you could go to see who could go the furthest without the hoop getting out of control.

Haymaking and Harvest.

Then the haymaking started. Most of the older boys had jobs leading horses while the wagons were loaded, or raking up the odd bits of hay and putting it on the next row. Nearly all the farmers' wives gave tea to the workers at haytime. As there were a lot of workers there were a lot of sandwiches to be cut and scones and cakes to be made. These were all carried to the field where the work was being done, so a lot more children were roped in to help carry the baskets of food. Their only pay was a chance to ride in an empty wagon, or ride the horses home at the end of the day. Haymaking often went on into September, then harvest followed straight away. The corn was cut with a binder pulled by three horses or sometimes a tractor. The sheaves were then "stooked" in sixes or eights and left to ripen before being carted and stacked, usually in the rickyard at the farm.

Then came the wild harvest- blackberries and crab apples for jams and puddings, elderberries, sloes and wild plums for wines. Often windfall apples were to be had if the farmer didn't make his own cider. What the family couldn't use the pig or hens could. Then there was the "gleaning" or "leasing". This was collecting the odd ears of corn that were left in the fields after the corn was carted.. This too helped feed the hens and pig.

About this time of year the conkers were ripe. All the children gathered conkers. There were all sorts of tricks which were supposed to make them tougher so they didn't break when your opponent hit them. Some put them in the bottom of the oven for several days, some pickled them in vinegar. When they were ready a hole was made through them and a piece of string about a foot long passed through the hole. Then you challenged one another to conker fights. The one who had first strike, was who could say this rhyme first,

"Obley, obley onker, my first conker!

Obley, obley O, my first go!"

While the conkers were still being played the wood had to be gathered for November 5th. Wood was valued a lot more then as nearly everyone had wood fires. A lot of the bonfires were made from hedge trimmings and, of course, elderwood. Very few country people will burn elder indoors as it's supposed to be unlucky. There always seemed to be a lot of old floor coverings a good way to get rid of them, and my word that old lino or oil cloth didn't half burn!

The children all went to bed much earlier then. There wasn't a lot to do except sit round a smoky fire and try to keep warm .You soon felt drowsy and realised the warmest place was in bed with a stone hot water bottle, or perhaps a brick warmed in the oven and put in an old sock.

Wildlife

I have always been interested in all things wild. Right from a child I liked to watch anything from mice to badgers. I would sit in the barn and watch mice and rats gnaw holes in sacks of feed, and then the cats creep up and grab them. As I got older I would sit in the wood and watch the rabbits playing. Several times I've seen a stoat rolling over and then lying down and waving his little legs in the air mesmerising a rabbit. When the rabbit got close enough the stoat would grab him behind the ears and that was the end for bunny! If you got there fairly quickly the stoat would run away and leave you the rabbit. It was always a nice fat one!

I have watched magpies going from nest to nest down a hedge. They must kill or break the eggs of hundreds of small birds a year. Although the hawks were persecuted up until about 1950 I had the pleasure of seeing most of them in the wild. The other birds which I saw a lot of at Swell Hill were corncrakes or landrails. One field in particular, the "Freeboard", always had some. When the corn was cut there would be 6 or 8 shot every year, besides the rabbits and hares. We ate the corncrakes roasted and they were very good. There were just as many again the next year. I don't think there are any left now. I think the modern farm machinery is as much to blame as the spraying.

I've always liked feeding game birds, making them go where I want them to, although I haven't shot for several years. I still feed the pheasants and partridges and I like to stand and watch them run to the feeding places, knowing that a bit of fresh corn would be there for them. Sometimes an an old cock will stand by the feed and keep all the others away. They're just like people.

Foxes

I am also very interested in foxes and badgers. We will take foxes first. Make no mistake, the fox is cunning. I have just recently witnessed a fox being attacked by a terrier and a lurcher. We thought it was dead. The dogs had left it and a man carried it some hundred yards to bring it home and bury it. He threw it over the gate into the farmyard, and the fox jumped up, ran a few yards, then stopped, looked round at us, and finally ran off as if nothing had happened.

I've also seen the hounds chase a fox into this village and lose the scent near the Manor gardens. Now we had seen a fox on several previous occasions on a summer house roof, among some ivy and other creepers. Well, the hunt was out and the huntsman gave the fox up and went down the field to Millais' wood, less than half a mile away. He had hardly got there when the fox peeped out over the ivy, listened for a minute or so, then hopped down and started mousing in some old hay where a sheep rack had been, pausing every now and then to look and listen. This was the hunted fox as he was covered in mud. There were two other people with me who witnessed this. The fox eventually saw us and trotted off to Gawcombe Woods.

Foxes do take lambs. I've seen them on several occasions, usually grabbing a tiny lamb when it's asleep, or when the ewe has two or three lambs and one wanders away from her. In the 1960s I witnessed something different. It was the beginning of April. We had just finished lambing and I had got 8 or 10 ewes with twins in the top field nearest home. To make it easier to count them, every morning I would take a bucket of feed for them. As soon as the ewes saw me they would run to the trough, then I could count them and their lambs. One morning in particular I was going out, so I fed the sheep very early, just as it was getting light. Well I put the food in the trough. One ewe spotted me. Then they all came. I counted the lambs several times and there was one missing. Then I heard a lamb bleating over the far side of the field. I walked along close to the hedge until I could see him. He was standing up stretching, and had obviously just woken up and didn't know where the rest had gone. Just then a fox ran across the field as fast as he could. He ran in a wide circle around the lamb, and then another circle closer. After doing four or five circles, just like a dog playing, he came in closer and grabbed the lamb by the back of the neck. I shouted and threw the feed bucket in his direction. He dropped the lamb and ran off.

The lamb lived, but always carried his head on one side. Now these lambs were about two weeks old and if I hadn't seen it I would never have guessed a fox would take a lamb at that age.

Another year, we had nearly finished lambing in early April. I was bringing the inlambers into the yard at night and, of course, any that had lambed during the day. Well, this evening there were two sets of twins born, so I carried two lambs and the mother followed as I brought the inlamb ewes in. I went straight back to fetch the other twins, but one lamb was gone and the mother was frantic, running to the hedge and then back to her remaining lamb, baa-ing all the time. I ran home and got my gun and just as I got back a fox was trying to grab the remaining lamb, with the ewe trying to fight it off. I had to pick my time but I shot the fox. She was a fairly old vixen, full of milk. She obviously had a litter of cubs just in the neighbouring wood. She wasn't satisfied with one lamb. She was going to take both for her cubs!

Badgers

I have been aware of badgers since I was very young. Grandad used to catch them in snares. He would bend a young ash sapling over and peg it down. The snare was attached to this in such a way that when the badger was caught in the ash tree it sprung back upright and Brock was strangled immediately. There were a lot of badgers at Swell Hill and it was necessary to thin them out as they killed a lot of poultry. Before anyone thought of deep litter houses most laying hens were kept in wooden poultry houses which were on small iron wheels and were moved about the farm so the hens were on fresh ground. In the autumn they would be put on the stubble to feed off the odd grains of corn that were dropped and of course they ate a lot of the pests which we now have to spray against. Now these hens would be shut in their houses at dusk, to guard against the foxes. But a wooden hut was no deterrent to the badgers. I have seen a poultry house door torn off its hinges by a badger and most of the hens killed. I was always told that a badger will eat anything a pig will eat. Well, a pig will eat anything from a rat or mouse to fruit and vegetables. It will eat any meat, including other pigs. When they are hungry badgers will bite lambs' heads off and just eat the head. When a badger kills a lamb he almost always takes it from the front. He holds his head on one side and bites the lamb's head off in one chop. I've never known the badger touch the rest of the body.

During the war years I would go badger digging with a gentleman who kept a pub at Moreton-in-Marsh. He was a kind old man who bred terriers as a pastime. He knew more about the habits of badgers than anyone else I've known. He didn't like his dogs to attack the badger. In fact, if one of his terriers got bitten by a badger he wouldn't bring him again. He would say, "That dog hasn't got many brains or he'd keep further away". His dogs were supposed to bark at a badger anything up to three or four feet away. Then, as long as they kept barking, you knew where to dig. The dogs that worked too close to their quarry were usually sold to foxhunts. I remember being with him one day when his dog was interested in a large rabbit hole, some hundred yards from a large badger sett. Charlie said, "If there is a badger in there he's got something the matter with him. The others have thrown him out of the main sett". Sure enough, when we dug him out he was very thin and weak. I now wonder if he had T.B. They now say badgers have T.B. and give it to the cows. I wonder if the cows give it to the badgers, as they love rooting in dry cow pats!

Badgers, along with otters, are my favourite animals. When I get the chance to watch them in the spring and autumn, I see them bringing their bedding out to dry. They usually walk backwards, dragging the bedding with their front feet, using them like garden rakes. On one occasion here at Westcote I saw a badger taking his bed in in the evening. He was not getting on very well, so he suddenly stood up on his back legs, grabbed the straw etc in his arms and walked two or three yards to the hole, carrying his bed like a person!

In my opinion there are far too many badgers for their own good. I would think there are at least five times as many now in the Cotswolds as there were before the war. One day they may get a disease which will wipe them out if there are too many. The Ministry of Agriculture are live-trapping them, testing them for diseases such as T.B. and then releasing them again. A friend who owns a small estate on the Gloucestershire-Herefordshire border told me that the Ministry asked his permission to catch badgers on his land. After a week or so they told him they'd caught 12 badgers and 5 of them had signs of T.B. He asked what they'd done with them and was told they'd let them go again where they'd caught them! You see there is a £1000 fine if you kill a badger, so I think in the end the badger will be the loser.

Changes in the countryside
due to the protection of predators

I have seen a big change in the countryside over the past fifty years. There were ten times as many song birds when I was a boy. It was unusual to see a magpie or jay, as they, along with other predators, were shot and trapped. If you were out with a gun looking for a rabbit or pheasant for dinner and you saw a magpie or jay you were expected to shoot it in preference to the rabbit. Now very few people except game keepers bother to shoot them. The farmers are being blamed for the lack of song birds because people think it's the sprays that kill them. It's not. It's the do-gooders who are protecting the sparrow hawks in particular. A sparrow hawk kills at least one song bird a day, more when it has young to feed. I supose there are between five and ten thousand sparrow hawks in the country so it doesn't bear thinking about.

No country person wants to wipe out any bird or animal completely, just to keep the population under control. We have done this successfully for hundreds of years, but now, with new rules and regulations, some of which come from a man sitting at a desk in Brussels, we are going to lose most of our small song birds, such as the linnet and goldfinch and perhaps the song thrush.

My Life in Westcote
Now me, and my life in Westcote and working at the Manor.

Well, I started work on a Monday morning. Arthur Rowland told me that the Captain had bought a roller at a sale about four miles away and my first job was to fetch it with the Ferguson tractor, but there was a snag! It was a horse drawn roller with shafts, so it would not fit easily on a tractor. So would I go and see Mr. Ernest Simmonds who had what was called an iron horse. This was a pole which fitted between the shafts with a drawbar at the end, thus converting horse drawn implements to be used with a tractor. Then I was to see Jim Griffin, because he had bought a horse rake at the same sale and perhaps I could tow that home for him at the same time. This was when I realised how neighbourly everyone was and it was more like the life I was used to at Swell Hill.

In all of the 48 years I have worked for Captain Millais he has never given me an order to do something. His usual words are "I wonder if you could do so and so for me". That would be the most urgent message. After working here for a while with no-one giving me orders I was quite happy to work after 5 o'clock or weekends without extra pay because I knew I could have any time off I wanted. I have stopped the tractor on many occasions to follow the hounds the rest of the day.

The second year I was here was a wet summer and haymaking was difficult. I had cut some meadow hay at the end of July and was not able to get it dry enough to carry.

The Captain came to me one day and said "Would you like to come to Derbyshire grouse shooting with me?" I thanked him and said I ought to stay at home and try to get the hay in. His reply was "Don't worry about the hay. We will have nice weather when we come back". Sure enough we did. The hay was bone dry and was not at all bad considering it had been cut for about three weeks.

Sheep

About 1953 we decided to have some sheep, so Church Piece was planted with turnips and kale, and a local dealer supplied about fifty old ewes. He delivered them late one evening and I didn't see them until the next morning. I was very disappointed. They were all breeds, sizes, shapes and colours. I did my best with them. We lost several and I think they produced about 30 lambs. That was a thankless job shepherding them! As time went on I introduced some better ewes into the flock, and after a few years we had quite a nice flock of mostly scotch half breeds. The drawback to our sheep farming was that we had nowhere near home to lamb them, as Arthur Rowland rented the building and the two fields near home, where he and his wife milked a few cows. So it meant making a lambing shelter somewhere down the fields, with no lighting and no water on tap. So I would visit them after tea and if one looked like lambing I would get down in the straw and stay half the night. On the other hand, if all was quiet when I visited I would come home to bed and get up at 3 or 4 in the morning and stay till it was light so that I could come home to breakfast.

Sawing wood

I have done a lot of small building jobs in and around the Manor with the Captain's help. We also did a lot of wood sawing. The Captain bought one of the first chainsaws. It was a two man machine with handles at both ends. It was heavy and dangerous. When the chain broke, which it did quite often, it usually wrapped itself around the legs of one or the other of us. The captain would help me most of the day, then go into his studio and paint until late at night.

Leisure Pursuits

Life was not all work. I was still playing football for Bledington, and playing some darts at the pub, and I spent a lot of time with my gun shooting pigeons and rabbits. I also kept ferrets and most Sunday mornings in the winter I went ferreting. About once a week we would go out with the long net after rabbits. I have heard of very large numbers being caught in a hundred yard net, but the most I ever had was about 12. One evening we set the long net up near Bould Wood where there were hundreds of rabbits. I knelt beside the net while my two mates walked round the far end of the field to drive the rabbits in. Well, it was a cloudy, windy night. Ideal we thought for netting, but the moon suddenly appeared from behind the clouds, lighting up everything. The rabbits ran in by the dozen, but they could see the net and they all jumped it except two. It was so light I could see the rabbits coming and I could see the two beaters at the other end of the field. By the time we had finished cursing and laughing the clouds had covered the moon again and it was pitch black.

The long net belonged to Arthur Rowland. It was made of silk and very old. Once we had set it up where Millais Wood is now. I was kneeling near it with my hand resting on the top to tell if we had caught anything when the net suddenly disappeared! I quickly shone my torch and it was a badger! I managed to grab the end of the net. The badger kept going and between us we tore the net to pieces! We never did find some of it. It was so old I don't suppose it worried the badger much. That was the end of our long netting!

Captain Millais had a marvellous lurcher called Amber. She would catch rabbits for fun. I remember taking her down the fields one afternoon and she caught 13 rabbits, which I carried home threaded on a stick. She caught most of them with cunning. she knew where all the holes and burrows were. If she could see a rabbit out feeding she would slink very low to the ground until she reached the hole. Then she would show herself. The rabbits would run straight towards her and she would have two or three of them. I saw her chase a hare through a gate. The hare went through the bottom of the gate and Amber went over the top and landed close enough to grab him. She was first cross greyhound and lassie collie. I have never known another dog so intelligent or so fast.

Motor Cycles and Cars

When I came to Westcote I had an Autocycle as my transport and I must say it never let me down. Then I bought a Royal Enfield motor cycle which I had for about a year. Then I saw a Morris Minor car advertised in the paper at £45. I bought it. It was a 1932 two seater. We had great fun with it. Just before my brother Reg left for New Zealand we went camping together. We took a tent and primus stove and what we could get in, or on, the little car. We started down by Bognor Regis, then followed the south coast to Weymouth and Bournemouth, then right along to Torquay and Lands End. We came back up the west coast to Porlock, Minehead and Weston. It took us about two weeks.

I had passed my driving test at the second attempt. The only time I put L plates up was when I went to Oxford for the tests. I was very lucky. I had been lucky with my little car so I started looking down the adverts for other cheap cars. Some I bought, repaired them a bit and sold them at a pound or two profit. You see there was no M.O.T. then, so as long as the steering and brakes worked you were O.K. I had bought and sold several cars when I acquired a Wolsley Wasp. This was a good car. It was unique with pump-up seat cushions. I kept this one and sold my little Minor for £35. I suppose it would be worth £2000 today!

I got caught once, good and proper. A man was sitting in a Vauxhall car out in the road one summer evening. He had the window down and as I walked by he spoke. So I stopped for a chat. He told me that he was doing a taxi job and was waiting to take a fare back to Cheltenham. We got talking about cars and he said the one he was driving was for sale. I made him an offer to which he agreed. I was to go back to Cheltenham with them and then I could have the car straight away. So I went to Cheltenham, paid him the money, and collected the documents and the car. I was very pleased with myself. I cleaned the car and the upholstery, and polished it. Then I advertised it in the local paper. As soon as the advert appeared two men came to my door. "You've got a Vauxhall car advertised", they said. "Yes," I agreed "Come and see it". They followed me to where the car was and looked round it. Then one man turned to me and said "I'm Detective So and So, and this is Mr. So and So of the Lombard Finance Company. This car was bought on hire purchase less than a week ago from a Cheltenham garage and it is the Finance Company's property". I said "What happens now?" they said "We don't let the car out of our sight, but the man you bought it from is in custody on another charge. He has no money, so our best advice is to forget it and put it down to experience". I think I learnt my lesson!

When the M.O.T. testing came in it stopped my part time car dealing, so, as I mentioned before, I started buying scrap cars and M.O.T. failures and cutting them up for scrap. There was not much money in this, but I met a lot of characters. One man I sold scrap cars to would fill the petrol tanks with water and put bricks and stones under the seats. This all added to the weight when he sold them at so much a ton over a weigh bridge! I had a lorry for a while and took my own scrap into Swindon, but they paid me less per ton than their regular suppliers, so it wasn't worth doing. I also had a go collecting wastepaper and cardboard. This was no good . They paid about £20 per ton. It takes a lot of paper to weigh a ton!

Family Life

We'd better go back a few years now to 1962, when Mary and me were married. My mother was crippled with arthritis and had difficulty in getting about the house. Mary kindly agreed to share this cottage, which was difficult at times. Her parents were then living at Bourton-on-the-Hill and Mary had been doing home help work there. I took her home to see her parents once or twice a week. The following year Tom was born. Things seemed to get easier then.

We never went out in the evenings together. I sometimes went to the pub on a Tuesday evening with an old friend, Jack Harding. We didn't drink much. We liked to play "spoof", sitting at the long table just inside the door, often with the landlord and his wife, Don and Audrey. Mary would occasionally go to Bingo with some friends.

My mum passed away at home in 1964 and was buried along with Dad at Swell. Not long after Mary's mum died from a heart attack, and her dad would come and stay with us from time to time.

When Tom started school Mary went to work at the Manor, part-time. This helped the funds a bit and took Mary's mind off her little boy at school! We managed to take a holiday in about 1970 and went to Butlins at Bognor Regis with some friends, where we really enjoyed ourselves. Then, two years later, we went to Minehead with the same gang. We had a caravan holiday in the Lake District two or three years later. We are not really holiday people. We prefer to sleep in our own beds. We have been away for odd weekends and we did rent a cottage in the Lakes last year, where we spent a week with our good friends, Garner and Anne,-more about them later.

The Village Hall

In the 1960s it was decided to repair the Tithe Barn at Church Westcote and make it into the village hall. A piece was built at the rear of the original barn to house the kitchen, cloakrooms and toilets. The fund raising fell to the committee and a few helpers. They did very well, but there was still about £3000 owing in the late seventies. I was invited on to the committee and, with Rosemary Coombs as secretary, we set about raising some big money. With the Millais' permission we held caravan rallies on Church Piece, together with a pig roast and various side shows. We almost cleared the debt with the bank. There was something in the region of £300 still owing. After asking me which bank the Village Hall used Mrs. Kay Millais gave me a letter for the manager. The Village Hall debt was cleared. We can only assume who paid it off.

Around this time I started a Youth Club in the Village Hall one evening a week and a Table Tennis Club on another evening. These were both successful. The Youth Club took in boys and girls from the surrounding villages, between the ages of 8 and 18. The Table Tennis Club took some adults as well. We played other villages and had some happy evenings. The late Basil Acock helped me a lot in the running of these clubs and also with transport for away games.

At about the same time I started a foot ball team. We had a pitch on Church Piece-the field above the cemetry, belonging at that time to Captain and Mrs. Millais. It wasn't long before we had two teams, 12 and under, and a senior team, 13 to 17. We had boys from surrounding villages. We joined the Bourton and District League, and our very first game was away in Northleach, which we lost, something like 13 to 1. We improved. Three years later we came top of the League, beating Northleach in the Final, 2 to 1. I still have the shield. As my son Tom grew older I thought I would give the Youth Club and football up, but no-one else would take it on! Who knows? Perhaps someone will devote a bit of time to the youngsters again. A few years ago Tony Gibson and one or two others started a cricket team which was great fun but it fell through lack of support. Perhaps we can blame T.V., or is just too much effort needed?

Renting the farm for ourselves

Mrs. Millais decided she would like to let the farm in 1983. As Tom had just finished at Hartbury College I decided to try my luck. I managed to rent the farm, as long as I helped her with the gardens two or three days a week. It meant a lot of hard work and a drop in income, but we had a go! We planted some barley and bought a couple of cows, one of which I milked in the mornings for our own use, and let calves suck the other. Although it was time consuming it worked quite well. We also went to Dorchester Sheep Fair and bought ten pedigree Dorset Horn ewes and a ram. This was the start of our Westcote flock of Dorset sheep, which we have been told is among the top ten flocks of Dorsets in this country.

Tom was married about this time and lived at Shipston-on-Stour, working for his father-in-law two days a week, so this left me with more to do. Tom and Deb had one daughter, Victoria, but I'm afraid the marriage didn't last and Tom came home, so was able to do a bit more on the farm.

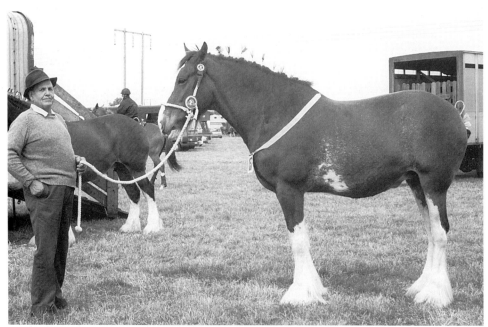

1993 Moreton Show. Lena, Best Mare in Show

Horses in Westcote

As I mentioned before I've always had a passion for horses. Well, all the time I worked for the Millaises they allowed me to keep a horse, sometimes two or three, which I would try to sell at a small profit. When Tom was about four we bought him a Shetland pony which he rode sometimes. But Shetlands are not the best riding ponies as they walk in very quick short strides, so we sold Lucky and bought larger ponies. The last one Tom had to ride was Walter, a heavy cob, which we broke to harness as well and we had a lot of fun with him. Then, when we started working for ourselves in 1983, we bought a pedigree shire mare and her foal. The first year we had her she took third prize at Moreton Show. We caught the showing bug then and I went down to Taunton and bought another shire mare, Lena, which we still have.

About this time we were selling our fat lambs at Stratford market and I got talking to a gentleman there, Garnet Parker, who helps pen the sheep. Now I found out that Garnet had two shires and, like me, he had worked them when he was young and they were in his blood. I told him that I was taking my horses to a show the following Saturday and invited him to come. He met us on the showground. He helped groom the horses and wash their legs, and I couldn't help noticing how quiet and calm the horses were. I asked him if he would show Lena for me. He agreed. As he was leading Lena into the ring I handed him a short whip which most show people carry. After going a few yards he came and gave me the whip back. "I wont carry a whip if you don't mind,"he said "It worries the old girl". He had noticed in that short time that Lena was looking at the whip instead of showing herself off. They won the championship that day and have done so many times since. It's quite uncanny. If Lena sees Garnet or hears his voice she calls out to him. He is a very interesting man to talk to and very knowledgeable about all animals. He breeds a foal most years from one of his mares and before they are very old they are following him about and he is picking their feet up and they love him. He always has a good sheep dog which you hardly ever hear him speak to. It seems to know just what he wants. Is there such a thing as an invisible thread between a man and an animal? Garnet and Anne are among our best friends, most genuine and interesting people. We were talking about a mutual friend one day, who is a bit of a "knowall". Whatever you tried to tell him he already knew. Garnet said "He's one of those people who are born with all the knowledge they'll ever need!"

1995 Westcote Lena & Blossom. Blossom from my original shire 'Dawn'.

Back to the horses. I bought Lena from a dealer. He phoned me after I had made an an appointment to see her. "I hope I'm not wasting your time", he said, "This mare's a bit thin, but I think she'll come right." Well, I bought the mare. She did "come right"!

Two years later I entered her for the Peterborough Show, which is the top Shire Horse Show in the world. We went the night before. Jim, his brother, Robert, and myself slept in the lorry and it was freezing! Lena had a lovely stable with all the mod cons! When we were getting her ready the next morning a man came to the stable "Well, well", he said "I never expected to see her again, especially here! I owned her at one time, she's a lovely mare". "Why did you sell her then?" I asked. "Oh," he said, "She had trouble foaling- had to have a caesarean, and, to be honest I thought she was going to die". Lena didn't win at Peterborough but I am very proud of her. She is here for the rest of her life and I think she appreciates it. We have four heavy horses now. We had eight at one time. They all do some work. We have a Wiltshire Dray, which we show with Prince and Boxer, and another horse called Duke, who is a good worker and, of course, the lovely Lena.

Latter days at Westcote

In 1985 Mrs. Millais died suddenly. We carried on renting the farm but the agents are no longer Tayler and Fletcher of Stow, but a London firm of solicitors. All they understand is collecting the rent. Westcote Manor was left in trust to Mrs. Millais' grandchildren, with the Captain living there for as long as he needs it. We grassed most of the Manor's flower gardens to make more lawns with a few small borders here and there, so I was able to keep it fairly tidy in two days a week with the Captain's help.

Gladys St. Roas, who lived next door to us, had worked at the Manor for about fifty years and Mary was helping her. It worked very well. The Manor has some twelve rooms so they had their work cut out, what with cooking as well as cleaning, but the Captain is a wonderful gentleman and a pleasure to do anything for. Well, Gladys had a fall when she was eighty and broke her arm. Although she was willing, she didn't come back to work at the Manor. She now lives with her daughter, Maxine, at Oddington. Mary and I visited her recently on her 86th birthday, and are pleased to say she is happy and well. Mary still looks after the Captain with the help of Caroline, Tom's partner, who is a lovely girl. I always admire anyone who will work, and Cas does. Although they have a little boy, Ben, who is now three, Caroline does relief milking, sells Avon products from door to door, helps at the Manor, and still finds time to help on the farm.

We had a setback this last twelve months. I was taken ill on 19th November 1996 and taken to Cheltenham Hospital, where I had a stomach operation. I came out for Christmas, but was in bed all the time and felt awful. The doctors and district nurses were wonderful. One or another would visit me every day, but the operation site did not heal. Through having blood tests they found that I had leukaemia so I was back in hospital on February 4th for treatment and came out on August 2nd. I cannot praise all the staff enough, and also my family, especially Mary, who visited me every day. Although she doesn't drive someone brought her in. If it wasn't Caroline or Tom it was my friend, Jim Ruck, or one of our many friends from all walks of life. How kind most people are when you are really up against it!

I'm not able to do much work yet, which is why I decided to jot down a few of my thoughts and memories.

Some people I have known

I must mention some of the wonderful people, past and present, it has been my pleasure to know. When I came to Westcote one of the people I saw most of was old Fred Newman, who lived opposite. I could listen to him for hours. He told me when he was a boy he went to work for Doctor Jay who then lived at the Manor. It was then over 1000 acres as Manor Farm, Nether Westcote went with it, and Dr. Jay employed a lot of men. He was an ex military man and was almost feared by his men. On Saturday the men all lined up in the stable yard to be paid, the head man first, the boys last. Well, Fred said it was his first week working and he was so proud when he lined up for his two and sixpence (twelve and a half pence now!). The Doctor had shot several rabbits that week so when he paid the head carter he said "Would you like a rabbit?" "No thank you Sir" was the reply. The doctor went down the line paying each man and asking if he wanted a rabbit. The reply was always the same "No thank you Sir". Well, Fred thought when he gets to me I'm going to have a rabbit. The Doctor got to Fred , gave him his two and sixpence and said "Would you like a rabbit Newman?" "Yes please", he said, "Right you are", he says "Here's your rabbit. Now give me sixpence back". The head carter said "Now you know why we says 'no' to his rabbits. He always charges us sixpence for them. We can catch his rabbits any time for nothing."

Old Fred had a small black dog named Paul who he took everywhere with him. Now Paul hadn't got a growl or a bad thought in his head. He wagged his tail and was pleased to see everyone, but Fred always kept him on a strong chain and said "I has to be careful with him. The missus will give him them raw beef bones and he gets as savage as a bear!".

Will Simms was another character worth listening to if you had a sense of humour. He was telling me one day that when he was a boy there was a big oak tree up in the allotment field. "So what happened to it?" I said. "Well, I'll tell you", said Will "There were a lot of crows eating the corn and in them days people used bird lime to catch song birds. They spread it on the branches and the birds stuck to it. Well, the farmer got so fed up with these crows that he covered this oak tree with lime. So these crows all settled in the oak tree and when the farmer went near them they all spread their wings and tried to fly. Well, being stuck to the tree, they uprooted it. The last we saw of them they was flying towards Stow taking the tree with them!"

I was talking to him about turnips and swedes one day. "Of course turnips ain't so big as they used to be", he says "I remember when I was a boy, the shepherd at the Manor lost a ewe and her two lambs. Well, they searched everywhere and when they did find them they had gnawed a hole in a turnip and they was inside, asleep!"

There was a man who worked at Gawcombe called Ron. He was what used to be called a day labourer. He was a good hedge layer and ditcher. He used to dig some ditches at night and weekends on what we called piece work - that was so much per yard or chain. Now Ron was one of the hardest workers I've known, but he loved his cider. When he dug the ditch between our farm and Gawcombe he did that on piece work. One Saturday afternoon he had been to the pub and brought home with him several bottles of rough cider. He stood three of these down the ditch at about five yard intervals. I was out with the gun and stopped to have a word with him. "I can't stop talking", he said "I've marked my afternoon's work out. Each time I gets to a bottle I shall sit down and empty it. When I've had the third I shall go home!"

Another man was a Romany gipsy named Wiggy Smith. Now I had a good child's pony for sale. She was a lovely pony and good with children, but if you let her go in a field it would take several people to catch her. Well, Wiggy told me one day that he knew a farmer who wanted a pony for his grandchildren and asked if he could take mine for the children to try. He came back the next day and gave me the money, saying the children had both ridden her and were thrilled to bits. I asked if he had told them that she was a job to catch. Wiggy thought for a moment. "Well," he said "They will find that out. There is no need to tell people anything they will find out, cause if it's something they will never find out, you no need to tell them anyway!"

Another great character was Darkie Robinson who I have mentioned earlier. He had some sheds down Gibsons' fields where he spent most evenings and weekends. I have spent many, many happy hours, along with others, just watching him mend things. Perhaps he would be putting new pistons in somebody's car or motor cycle. Then someone would bring him a kettle, or some other household object, to be soldered. He would also make chrystal radio sets with an empty vim carton, a knob of coal and a few twists of copper wire. Later, he would be mending radios and TVs. All the time he would have a woodbine going and be laughing and joking.

I remember a garage proprietor bringing him a motor cycle all in pieces. He brought it in a bath. There was also some water in the bottom! "Can you help me out?" the garage man said "Someone brought this bike in about a year ago. We pulled it to pieces. We didn't see the owner again till yesterday. He expected it to be repaired." Darkie said "If it's all there give me about a week." Sure enough, about a week later, after making some bits and pieces, he said "Come in the other shed. We will try her." After quite a bit of kicking she fired up in a cloud of smoke. Darkie sat down on an upturned box, watched it for a few minutes, then switched it off and wandered back into his workshop and started mending something else. You see he got great satisfaction from repairing things. I thought it was a mammoth task done in record time. He didn't. He looked on it as another job that wanted doing.

He was also a good plumber. I would think he mended something or other in every house in Westcote, often an emergency at short notice. I remember a man from Fifield fetching him one Christmas morning. He and his family had come home that morning and found the house flooded. Darkie went and repaired the burst pipe, although he'd never seen the family before. He said "Poor people. Fancy having that happen to you on Christmas Day!" I'm sure he never thought of the inconvenience to himself! What a great man, who sadly is no longer with us.

Summing up

I am sixty seven now and I have seen a lot of changes. I also think I lived in a good period. I don't think the next fifty years will be so happy or interesting. Times were harder when I was young. Children went to school with patches on their clothes and perhaps only one pair of shoes to their name. I don't think this made a bit of difference to their health or happiness. Our heads were not filled with T.V. adverts or "Top of the Pops" or all the violent programmes. Children, on the whole, learnt more things that would help them in later life. The girls learnt to knit and sew and to cook simple dishes before they were twelve or thirteen. By the time they were sixteen they had learnt from their mothers all the basics of housekeeping. The boys would be much the same. They learnt the basics of woodworking and gardening while still at school. They spent most weekends helping their fathers, who would perhaps be carpenters, wallers or maybe a blacksmith or woodman. When not helping their fathers they would be working on farms or in gardens. By the time they left school these boys knew how to work and would be partly skilled in the job of their choice. Now, plenty of these young people leaving school at sixteen or seventeen don't know anything about everyday life, although they can tell you about fax machines and computers. The day may come again when common sense will be the thing that's needed to fill our bread baskets!

Leisure used to mean sitting outside in the summer, reading the paper, or chatting to friends; in the winter, dozing by the fire or perhaps sitting in the Local. Now people are told that they have more leisure time, but have they? They rush home from work to clean the car, or drive ten miles or so to the supermarket. Most have a lawn to cut once or twice a week. Then there seems to be endless painting and decorating. Then there's the endless driving to visit friends and relations. You must remember to do the football pools, buy a lottery ticket, perhaps drive the boys to a football or cricket match, maybe a hundred miles away. None of this is leisure! These are all jobs that other people are paid to do. You can't relax when you're driving. I think we are all being conditioned into thinking we have things easier. I doubt it!

1996 Westcote. Me, my grandson Ben and my son Tom.

"the lands I seldom left"

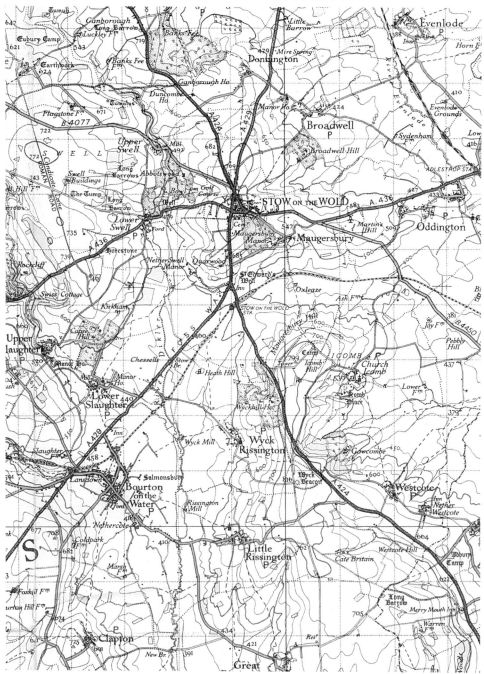

Small section of old Ordnance Survey 1 inch map sheet 144, Cheltenham and Evesham. 1930 with later corrections published 1946.